STEPPING STONES

— TO —
Recovery

STEPPING STONES TO Recovery

by Bill Pittman

© 1988 by Glen Abbey Books, Inc.

All rights reserved
Published by:
  Glen Abbey Books, Inc., Seattle, Washington
  1-800-782-2239
  1-206-548-9360

Printed and bound in the United States of America
First Edition   Fifth Printing
Cover Design by Michelle Ogata, Graphiti Associates, Inc.,
  Seattle, WA

Library of Congress Cataloging-in-Publication Data

Pittman, Bill
  Stepping stones to recovery.

  1. Alcoholics—Rehabilitation—United States.
2. Alcoholism—United States—Psychological aspects.
3. Alcoholism—Spiritual aspects—Christianity. I. Title.
HV5279.P58 1988   362.2'928   87-73389
ISBN 0-934125-04-X

Disclaimer: The publication of this volume does not imply affiliation with nor appproval or endorsement from Alcoholics Anonymous World Services, Inc.

10 9 8 7 6 5

This Book Is Gratefully Dedicated

To

12th Step Workers,
Past, Present, and Future.

PREFACE

The purpose of *Stepping Stones To Recovery* is to bring together ideas and ideals of the spiritual wisdom of the Twelve Step Program of Alcoholics Anonymous. I have been working on an annotated bibliography of the writings from and about Alcoholics Anonymous. While researching articles, books, pamphlets, journals, newsletters, etc., I became aware of the most frequently mentioned subject areas that non-AA and AA members write about. It is probably not surprising that these areas center around spirituality, and those subjects have formed the chapter headings for this anthology. By including a number of articles on each subject, a "group conscience" is reached which gives perspective and understanding to these major topic areas: Acceptance, Spirituality, Surrender, Prayer and Meditation, Slogans, and Prayers.

This compilation is not intended to replace or compete with the "Big Book," *12x12*, and literature from AA Headquarters, but to join other "helpful books" that AAs and members of various 12 Step Programs may choose to read.

While Nell Wing, AA's first archivist and long-time secretary to Bill W., was researching the origins of the Serenity Prayer she wrote: "In any case, the Serenity Prayer, for almost forty years now, has become so deeply imbedded, so closely woven into the fabric, into the very tapestry of AA thinking, living, and into its philosophy that it's difficult to remember it did not originate from AA headquarters itself." This is also true of many of the articles, slogans, and prayers that follow, which have been reprinted and repeated so often the original author and source is unclear. Every effort has been made to find this information, give proper credit, and secure copyright permission when necessary.

The articles from the non-AAs Shoemaker, Silkworth, and Tiebout are included to add yet another dimension to the topics of this volume. More important are the outstanding writings of the women and men who are together "fellow travelers" on the spiritual path of recovery as suggested by the Alcoholics Anonymous Program. Here, then, is a treasury of articles, slogans, and prayers . . . *Stepping Stones To Recovery.*

ACKNOWLEDGMENTS

I wish to thank the following individuals for their assistance in the preparation of this book: Mel B., Larry B., Franklin B., Pat B., Cecil C., Virginia Cone, Lynda Ernst, Elizabeth Garcia, Jack A.H., Peter L., Frank M., Curtis M., Ciaran O'Mahony, Doreen Quintana, Julie R., Connie S., Naomi Strassberg, Henry Williams III, Julia Willinger, Sheryl Feldinger, and Nell Wing.

It is with gratitude that I thank the following individuals for their cooperation in granting permission to reprint various articles: Joan A., Ginny A., Elise D., Doug D., Clare F., Isabel G., Donna G., Geraldine Howell, Colby H., Ruth Ann H., David H., Madeline Jordon, Arnie Keuning, Anne M., Gerrie M., Bob Morris, Merl M., Janet N., Linda Peterson, Al R., Helen R., Shep R., Bill S., Helen Shoemaker, Morris S., Robert W., Cathy W., and Imogene Z.

TABLE OF CONTENTS

I. ACCEPTANCE

II. SPIRITUALITY

III. PRAYER AND MEDITATION

IV. THE SERENITY PRAYER

V. PERSONAL SHARING

VI. THE REVEREND CANON SAMUEL M. SHOEMAKER

VII. WILLIAM DUNCAN SILKWORTH, M.D.

VIII. WILLIAM GRIFFITH WILSON

IX. HARRY TIEBOUT M.D.

X. RICHMOND WALKER

XI. SLOGANS

XII. PRAYERS

XIII. STEPS AND TRADITIONS

PERMISSIONS AND REFERENCES

WHY WE WERE CHOSEN

God in His wisdom selected this group of men and women to be the Purveyors of His goodness. In selecting them through whom to bring about this phenomenon He went not to the proud, the mighty, the famous, or the brilliant. He went instead to the humble, to the sick, to the unfortunate. He went right to the drunkard, the so-called weakling of the world. Well might He have said to us, "Unto your weak and feeble hands I have entrusted a power beyond estimate. To you has been given that which has been denied the most learned of your fellows. Not to scientists or statesmen, not to wives or mothers, not even to My priests or ministers have I given this gift of healing other alcoholics which I entrust to you.

"It must be used unselfishly; it carries with it grave responsibility. No day can be too long; no demands upon your time can be too urgent; no case be too pitiful; no task too hard; no effort too great. It must be used with tolerance for I have restricted its application to no race, no creed, and no denomination. Personal criticism you must expect; lack of appreciation will be common; ridicule will be your lot; your motives will be misjudged. You must be prepared for adversity, for what men call adversity is the ladder you must use to ascend the rungs toward spiritual perfection, and remember, in the exercise of this power, I shall not exact from you beyond your capabilities.

"You are not selected because of exceptional talents, and be careful always, if success attends your efforts, not to ascribe to personal superiority that to which you can lay claim only by virtue of My gift. If I had wanted learned men to accomplish this mission, the power would have been entrusted to the physician and scientist. If I had wanted eloquent men, there would have been many anxious for the assignment, for talk is the easiest used of all talents with which I have endowed mankind. If I had wanted scholarly men, the world is filled with better qualified men than you who would be available. You were selected because you have been the outcasts of the world and your long experience as drunkards has made or should make you humbly alert to the cries of distress that come from the lonely hearts of alcoholics everywhere.

"Keep ever in mind the admission you made on the day of your profession in AA, namely that you are powerless and that it was only with your willingness to turn your life and will unto My keeping that relief came to you."[1]

"Spirituality is at the heart of the Twelve Step program of recovery. There is not a spiritual part of the program. It *is* a spiritual program."

Jerry D.

I. ACCEPTANCE

AND ACCEPTANCE IS THE ANSWER...

And acceptance is the answer to *all* my problems today. When I am disturbed, it is because I find some person, place, thing, or situation—some fact of my life—unacceptable to me, and I can find no serenity until I accept that person, place, thing, or situation as being exactly the way it is supposed to be at this moment. Nothing, absolutely nothing happens in God's world by mistake. Until I could accept my alcoholism, I could not stay sober; unless I accept life completely on life's terms, I cannot be happy. I need to concentrate not so much on what needs to be changed in the world as on what needs to be changed in me and in my attitudes.[2]

THE ACCEPTANCE OF ONESELF

The acceptance of oneself is the essence of the moral problem and the epitome of a whole outlook upon life. That I feed the hungry, that I forgive an insult, that I love my enemy in the name of Christ—all these are undoubtedly great virtues. What I do unto the least of my brethren, that I do unto Christ. But what if I should discover that the least amongst them all, the poorest of all the beggars, the most impudent of all the offenders, the very enemy himself—that these are within me, and that I myself stand in need of the alms of my own kindness—that I myself am the enemy who must be loved—what then? As a rule, the Christian's attitude is then reversed; there is no longer any question of love or long-suffering: we condemn and rage against ourselves. We hide it from the world; we refuse to admit ever having met this least lowly in ourselves. Had it been God Himself who drew near to us in this despicable form, we should have denied Him a thousand times before a single cock had crowed.[29]

WHAT IS ACCEPTANCE?
By Bill W.

One way to get at the meaning of the principle of acceptance is to meditate upon it in the context of AA's much used prayer, "God grant me the serenity to accept the things I cannot change, courage to change the things I can, and the wisdom to know the difference."

Essentially this is to ask for the resources of Grace by which we may make spiritual progress under all conditions. Greatly emphasized in this wonderful prayer is a need for the kind of wisdom that discriminates between the possible and the impossible. We shall also see that life's formidable array of pains and problems will require many different degrees of acceptance as we try to apply this valued principle.

Sometimes we have to find the right kind of acceptance for each day. Sometimes we need to develop acceptance for what may come to pass tomorrow, and yet again we shall have to accept a condition that may never change. Then, too, there frequently has to be right and realistic acceptance of grievous flaws within ourselves and serious faults within those about us—defects that may not be fully remedied for years, if ever.

All of us will encounter failures, some retrievable and some not. We shall often meet with defeat—sometimes by accident, sometimes self-inflicted, and at still other times dealt to us by the injustice and violence of other people. Most of us will meet up with some degree of worldly success, and here the problem of the right kind of acceptance will be really difficult. Then there will be illness and death. How indeed shall we be able to accept all these?

It is always worthwhile to consider how grossly that good word acceptance can be misused. It can be warped to justify nearly every brand of weakness, nonsense, and folly. For instance, we can "accept" failure as a chronic condition, forever without profit or remedy. We can "accept" worldly success pridefully, as something wholly of our own making. We can also "accept" illness and death as certain evidence of a hostile and godless universe. With these twistings of acceptance, we AAs have had vast experience. Hence we constantly try to remind ourselves that these perversions of acceptance are just gimmicks for excuse-making: a losing game at which we are, or at least have been, the world's champions.

This is why we treasure our "Serenity Prayer" so much. It brings a new light to us that can dissipate our old-time and nearly fatal habit of fooling ourselves. In the radiance of this prayer we see that defeat, rightly accepted, need be no disaster. We know that we do not have to run away, nor ought we again try to overcome adversity by still another bull-dozing power drive that can only push up obstacles before us faster than they can be taken down.

On entering AA, we become the beneficiaries of a very different experience. Our new way of staying sober is literally founded upon the proposition that "Of ourselves, we are nothing, the Father doeth the works." In steps one and two of our recovery program these ideas are specifically spelled out: "We admitted that we were powerless over alcohol . . . that our lives had become unmanageable"—"Came to believe that a power greater than ourselves could restore us to sanity." We couldn't lick alcohol with our own remaining resources and so we accepted the further fact that dependence upon a Higher Power (if only our AA group) could do this hitherto impossible job.

The moment we were able to fully accept these facts, our release from the alcohol compulsion had begun. For most of us this pair of acceptances had required a lot of exertion to achieve. Our whole treasured philosophy of self-sufficiency had to be cast aside. This had not been done with old-fashioned will power; it was instead a matter of developing the willingness to accept these new facts of living. We neither ran nor fought. But accept we did. And then we were free. There had been no irretrievable disaster.

This kind of acceptance and faith is capable of producing 100 percent sobriety. In fact it usually does; and it must, else we could have no life at all. But the moment we carry these attitudes into our emotional problems, we find that only relative results are possible. Nobody can, for example, become completely free from fear, anger, and pride. Hence in this life we shall attain nothing like perfect humility and love. So we shall have to settle, respecting most of our problems, for a very gradual progress, punctuated sometimes by heavy setbacks. Our old-time attitudes of "all or nothing" will have to be abandoned.

Therefore our very first problem is to accept our present circumstances as they are, ourselves as we are, and the people about us as they are. This is to adopt a realistic humility without which no genuine advance can even begin. Again and again, we shall need to return to that unflattering point of departure. This is an exercise in acceptance that we can profitably practice every day of our lives. Provided we strenuously avoid turning these realistic surveys of the facts of life into unrealistic alibis for apathy or defeatism, they can be the sure foundation upon which increased emotional health and therefore spiritual progress can be built. At least this seems to be my own experience.

Another exercise that I practice is to try for a full inventory of my blessings and then for a right acceptance of the many gifts that are mine—both temporal and spiritual. Here I try to achieve a state of joyful gratitude. When such a brand of gratitude is repeatedly affirmed and pondered, it can finally displace the natural tendency to congratulate myself on whatever progress I may have been enabled to make in some areas of living. I try hard to hold fast to the truth that a full and thankful heart cannot entertain great conceits. When brimming with gratitude, one's heartbeat must surely result in outgoing love, the finest emotion that we can ever know.

In times of very rough going, the grateful acceptance of my blessings, oft repeated, can also bring me some of the serenity of which our AA prayer speaks. Whenever I fall under acute pressures I lengthen my daily walks and slowly repeat our Serenity Prayer in rhythm to my steps and breathing. If I feel that my pain has in part been occasioned by others, I try to repeat, "God grant me the serenity to love their best, and never fear their worst." This benign healing process of repitition, sometimes necessary to persist with for days, has seldom failed to restore me to at least a workable emotional balance and perspective.

Another helpful step is to steadfastly affirm the understanding that pain can bring. Indeed pain is one of our greatest teachers. Though I still find it difficult to accept today's pain and anxiety with any great degree of serenity—as those more advanced in the spiritual life seem able to do—I can, if I try hard, give thanks for present pain nevertheless. I find the willingness to do this when I contemplate the lessons learned from past suffering—lessons which have led to the blessings I now enjoy. I can remember, if I insist, how the agonies of alcoholism, the pain of rebellion and thwarted pride, have often led me to God's Grace, and on to a new freedom. So, as I walk along, I repeat still other phrases such as these, "Pain is the touchstone of progress" ... "Fear no evil" ... "This, too, will pass" ... "This experience can be turned to benefit." These fragments of prayer bring far more than mere comfort. They keep me on the track of right acceptance; they break up my compulsive themes of guilt, depression, rebellion, and pride; and sometimes they endow me with the courage to change the things I can, and the wisdom to know the difference.

To those who never have given these potent exercises in acceptance a real workout I recommend them highly the next time the heat is on. Or, for that matter, at any time![3]

DON'T LET THORNS
OBSCURE THE ROSES
Victory Over Problems

I was simply trying to assure Kathy, one year sober, that she must not be dismayed when problems rear their ugly heads during sobriety in Alcoholics Anonymous. I told her, "AA can't promise you a rose garden, just the same. We can enjoy the loveliest rewards only when we are vigilant in weeding, mulching, hoeing, fertilizing, watering, spraying, and pruning to cope with gardening problems. It's up to each of us. Nobody can care for our gardens for us."

This is about as fine a parable about handling problems in our AA lives that I've encountered to date.

It can be easy for any of us at any time to imagine that we luxuriate in a trouble-free existence now that we're sober. Free of the miseries, mental and physical, of constant intoxication, we may become too accustomed to happy peace of mind that we often begin to believe we are not supposed to ever have problems in AA.

By so deluding ourselves, we become unprepared to accept some living problems as natural. Small wonder that non-alcoholic problems can make us panic at the thought that we are retrogressing and in danger of a slip. It seldom occurs to us in such a mental state that if sober AA members never got zonked by troubles, there would be no need for groups that concentrate on problems in discussion meetings.

Problems don't befall sober AAs because they are alcoholics, but because they belong to the human race. Mankind always has had problems. The biggest problem in the world today just may be problems.

The primary problem begins with the fact that many men or women don't like being what they are.

We in AA invited growing problems when we decided we were powerless over alcohol, that our lives had become unmanageable, and that we were sick and tired of being sick and tired. It requires coping with our problems if we are to start making that 180 degree turn in character and behavior. We are told that nobody can make that change for us, but that we cannot make it alone.

So no member should shrink from laying out his problems for all to see. Holding them secretly inside prevents growth. Those who let it all hang out at a meeting are less likely to be headed for a drunk and more likely to be headed toward saving their own lives.

Our first big problem solution after sobriety can well be in learning that our individual destiny is living in the world as we find it.

Coping with life is solving our own problems. The farthest we can go outside of ourselves is caring and sharing with others.

Solutions are stepping stones to recovery. Every answer is a healer of wounds. Every breakthrough we achieve is another approach to self-confidence, knowledge, awareness, and growth.

With each victory over a problem while sober, we in AA fortify our gratitude. We never need to ask "how?" when we cope with problems; the Steps give us the answers to living with ourselves, the Traditions for living with others.

ACCEPTANCE OF OURSELVES
In AA There Is Hope

Upon arrival at AA, most of us know very little about ourselves, much less accept ourselves for what we really are. Our egos tell us "There's nothing wrong with me—everyone else is misguided."

As we work the Steps we begin to glimpse what we're really like and see selfishness, dishonesty, and other manifestations of our self-centered fear. We don't particularly like what we learn about our character and arrive at a turning point. Will we accept the truth and work on our defects or will we stop looking because it's too painful? Contented sobriety is the product of the former; dryness a result of the latter.

Acceptance comes through denial bargaining, anger, and depression. We deny there's anything wrong with us until it becomes too painful to blame the world and everyone in it for our trouble—we're forced to admit there's something wrong with us— not them. We try to bargain away what we don't like: "I wouldn't be so angry if you'd give me what I want, God." And anger manifests itself—who would dare suggest we're less than perfect? Our anger turns inward and becomes depression: "Woe is me, my life isn't worth living because I've got some things wrong with me."

In AA there is hope and a Step to work. No one ever said it was easy—accepting the truth has nothing to do with liking it—but if we try, we'll be a lot better than we used to be![30]

THE POWER OF ACCEPTANCE
Turning It Over

Many of my earlier memories are of trying very hard, with a small child's limited resources, to change the people, places, and things in my little life that were unacceptable to me. In fact, it seems that all my life I have pitted my strength and ingenuity against unacceptable situations, trying to change them into situations I could accept. The less they budged, the more frustrated I felt.

Even after I discovered alcohol's ability to erase situations unacceptable to me when sober—or to change my mood to fit into them—I was still faced with the hassle of having to sober up to struggle through unacceptable situations at home and at work. I became addicted to alcohol and to its illusion of power. It was the only agent of change I had. I also developed the stomach problems, backaches, tension headaches, and generally tense attitudes that define your basic Type A tilter at windmills.

I finally ran to the end of my own endurance and asked for help. My answer was Alcoholics Anonymous. I became free from alcohol but was faced once again with my old enemy, powerless over my life. I repeatedly heard and read in AA that we have to ask God for the serenity to accept the things we cannot change. I did, and would like to share the growth in acceptance that God has given me.

First I learned that I do not have to like something to accept it. I had assumed that in order to accept something, I had to condone it, agree with it, or otherwise change my attitude to conform with the position of the person, place, or thing. I found this unnecessary. It would not be growth for me to change to conform with some of the attitudes I encounter. It is growth, however, when I try to understand other people by listening to them, whether I agree with them or not. It is also growth when I admit to myself that I cannot change something or someone, and ask God for the courage to turn my thinking toward something I can change.

I have also learned that I do not have to choose something to accept it. I had come to believe that in order to accept something, I had to continue to allow it to be a part of my life. I've learned this is not true, either. I can accept certain people, places, or things exactly as they are, but still choose not to affiliate myself with them. I believe God does guide our choices when we turn our lives, and our wills over to him. I also believe that the power to choose is the only power I have.

I look at life now as if it were a cafeteria. I do not assume, when I get in line at a cafeteria, that everything offered there is for me. I am expected to make my choices from the selection offered. Do I criticize the roast beef simply because I'm in the mood for fish that day, or because my cholesterol is high and my physician recommends I avoid red meat? Perhaps the pie is unfitting for me because of obesity or diabetes, but do I have the right to say that pie is wrong for my friend who needs to add twenty pounds to her weight for her health's sake? By the same token, the career, life-style, or mate that may not be right for me may be perfect for the person sitting to my left at my next meeting.

Looking at things this way has freed me from having to justify to myself and to others my reasons for making certain choices. It forces me to be honest with myself about priorities. Most of all, it comforts me with the knowledge that God cares for me and my life and that, one day at a time, He is restoring me to sanity by granting me the serenity to accept those things I cannot change (but need to choose).[3]

ACCEPTING GUIDANCE
Stop Struggling With God

We listened to a qualification the other night at an AA meeting that was devoted to the Third Step and we realized that for many of us much time must pass before we can say in simple confidence, "The Lord is my Shepherd, I shall not want."

The great psalm of David is indeed a song of simple faith, which only those who do not struggle against the Supreme Power can sing.

And why do we struggle? Perhaps fear and worry cloud our vision and make us unwilling to let ourselves go. More likely, our faith is pride, which short-circuits our reason or else sends our minds into winding by-paths of involved thinking. With pride goes a quarrelsome spirit, which short-circuits the mind. Selfishness, too, blinds the vision and hides the path.

Some of us struggle not against the Supreme Power but with it. The harder we try to understand, the less we do understand. Success comes then when we quit struggling, when we relax and let ourselves see what there is to be seen.

Only a few of us, a very few of us, ever have a dramatic revelation of the existence of the Higher Power. Such revelations usually result from intensely emotional experiences. For most of us, there are no shafts of light, no voices in the sky, no seizures.

The Supreme Power reveals itself to us as we permit God to do so. But we who have sat so long in the seat of the scornful and walked in the paths of the ungodly do have to seek the Supreme Power and we do have to ask for guidance without mental reservation. The Supreme Power may be admitted to a mind cluttered with rubbish, since a beginning has to be made, but it will not abide in a mind that devotes itself to rubbish. Weeds will choke good seed, and all the more so if we continue to encourage the weeds.

First we have to seek. We may start by setting aside a part of each day for a period of quiet thought. Let us be alone, at such times, and let us set aside all contention, all fuming, all fretting. The first necessity is to quiet the mind, to shut out all thought until relaxation comes. If we get no farther than this at first, the mental quiet will help.

The next thing is to let the mind reach out, until it can find something upon which it can rest. For some of us, that something is the endless space that makes us feel the vastness of the universe. Some of us demand something more concrete and some demand an actual object of some sort, something inanimate or something of human form whose goodness and virtue we respect.

The Power that we seek is the source of all good; from it comes nothing evil. The Power is a strict judge of our honesty, of our acts. When we hold mental conversation with the Supreme Power we are brought to the line of absolute truth. Every evasion delays our finding rest, delays our finding the path to a New Way of Life. For those who continue to sit in the seat of the scornful, there is no help in AA. But those who will look for the help of a Higher Power will find it. Realization may come slowly at first, but it will come. We learn step by step, to accept the guidance of the Supreme Power.[4]

WHEN PAIN IS YOUR PARTNER
The Beginning Of Working The Program

As a recovering alcoholic you would imagine that I should be accustomed to pain and anguish. After all, I suffered through it more and more as my disease progressed. However, it's difficult now. You see, I don't choose to self-medicate through intoxication in order to relieve it. That never worked anyway. It always seemed to return, only in a much more severe form. Therefore, today I am forced to learn new, and much more effective ways to deal with any mental anguish that I may experience now.

But even though I choose not to drink today, I am still an alcoholic, and even though I am struggling towards spiritual growth, sometimes some of my old behavior patterns will return to haunt me. I then realize that many of my old defense mechanisms, such as denial, rationalization, and mainly the need (or want) to control, are only sublimated. I may even discover some new ones I never knew I possessed that I attempt to use, in vain, if the old ones aren't working.

Because I am so afraid to surrender what little I have, I find myself fighting my Higher Power from the beginning. It won't bother God because it is a fight that God is used to winning. The battle is all part of the process of learning to own my own limitations. I must remember that I have surrendered the desire to control my life and to start dealing with what I am able to do, not what I want to do.

Sometimes I yell impatiently, "I can't put up with this! My head feels it's on wrong." God answers, "That's because it is on all wrong." My mouth drops open. That's not the answer I expected. Instead, it is the truth. Because I do not trust myself I must trust my Higher Power. "Well," God says, "what are you waiting for? Get to work. Don't challenge what you can't change or you'll end up against a brick wall. Start by locating your limits and challenging those."

I suddenly arrive at the realization that I must backtrack and place much more energy into myself if I expect to begin growing again. Some days are going to be better than others. At times I'll be hurt, but I'll recover and start again. You see, pain and anguish are a problem because they numb everything. And, if your mind is not functioning appropriately, your program for growth will suffer. Now, everyone has pain. But pain can be evaluated. There are times when you can go through it and over it, times when you have to lie down and let it pass.

But first must come the **acceptance**. Once you accept a situation, no matter how painful it is, you can go around it and keep going. Secondly, there must be **hope**. Hope is a very active part of the healing process. If you have hope and really think you'll get better and never give up the desire, then you do have a good start.

Slowly, I am coming to the understanding that I am the enemy. Acceptance does not mean giving in or giving up. It is the real beginning of working the AA Program. I may not like my limitations, but I have finally accepted the fact that they belong to me.

I felt compelled to place these thoughts on paper because they remind me that the recovery process (and personal growth) is a life-long proposition. But as long as the AA Principles and Philosophy are followed, the quality of life does get better— **One Day At A Time**.[5]

ACCEPTING HUMILITY
Recovery Depends On It

Humility Is Relative

This is a point of view with which I disagree. Humility does not change with time: today's society cannot reduce humility and give us a little more of anything—wealth, acclaim, or ego. The contents of humility are not variables: being unpretentious, unassuming, modest, and decent; having the quality of "lowliness of mind" does not change with the times.

Humility—even after years of having been in the limelight as ego-tripping intellectuals, as businessmen who believed that they ran the show, or as legless drunks being pointed to in the street—does not mean fitting in once again.

Humility, as its definition suggests, means being able to see oneself as one is: and no one of us is as important as we make ourselves out to be. When I can truly see myself as the "nothing" that I am, then humility is strengthened. When all the gains of life and the crutches are removed, all that remains is that awareness of "nothingness"—without even a will of my own. On this "emptiness" alone can one build the life demanded of us by the Steps of AA.

Our First Step is admitting powerlessness, and the Second is to ask "elsewhere" for assistance: elsewhere than in the realms of that with which we were no longer able to cope.

Be Yourself

The existence of the humble asks nothing of others or of life itself but to carry on unhindered on a spiritual, hence non-materialistic, path. Yet today, asking for this kind of life can mean being put in the limelight once again: it is a request to be different: it is a rejection of the values that we are often forced to believe that we need. We can be noticeable trying to be humble as we had been noticeable in our drinking "extravaganzas."

Our drinking however, eventually pushed us so far down that no one bothered us too much; so also our humility, our life in reverse, should go unhindered. Whereas with drinking people avoided us for what we had become, so humility also can "push away" people—lest, perhaps, they might feel some of their worldly values to be excessive. Many, I believe, would like to be "simple" or modest, but can honestly see no reason to be so.

As alcoholics, and members of AA, we can see no reason to be other than humble: our sobriety today depends on our acceptance of a Way of Life that our non-alcoholic friends might laugh off as eccentric. The fact is that we know that our lives depend on it—and often we can see also that the lives of all men depend upon it.

To this alcoholic and AA member, humility means knowing that really I am nothing, and accepting that. Furthermore, it means trying, in some way, to let others—those who find life impossible as I once did—see that there is a contented existence in humility . . . . [6]

THE FREEDOM OF ACCEPTANCE
Dealing With Denial

Third Step: *Made a decision to turn our will and our lives over to the care of God as we understood Him.*

One of the big problems we have is a denial of all kinds of feelings. We don't want to look at what we see on the dark side of ourselves. They are the things we hide and spend a lot of our precious energy keeping hidden. We hide things and keep people away from us so they won't see our particular skeleton in the closet. There also can be a great denial of our feelings of anger and pain when we try to achieve peace. Surrender helps us in all this, by letting us accept all the things in us and around us as they are. We give up the struggle against the world, and then we are free to change the few things about us that we can change, that really need changing.

We like acceptance, and the best way I've found to get acceptance is to give it first. Then I usually find I get back the acceptance I need. Another thing I, or we, need to look at is surrender itself, so we can get a better understanding of that process. What is surrender? Is it ego or surrender? Living in ego means wanting what you don't have. Surrender means appreciating and being grateful for what you do have. Ego is when we constantly think we know what is best for us.

Surrender is when we see that the great stream of life, our Higher Power, or God as we understand Him, knows what is best for us. It is the prayer of release. Living the surrendered life is like being a butterfly, a soul in full flight seeking the beauties of life. Like the butterfly, we start putting our trust in the present good things instead of hoping for the next good thing. To get this attitude we need to seek a new vision, a new hope, a new spirit.[7]

CHANGES
Responsibility For Our Attitudes And Feelings

What a relief to allow others to be themselves. I then have time to work on me. This is a freedom the AA Program has given me.

I spent most of my life trying to change reality. People, places, and things were my problem (I thought). If only people would behave the way I wanted them everything would be okay. Of course people rarely cooperated, and I became frustrated and angry. I blamed them for my frustration and increased my efforts to change them. I became extremely confused, angry, and resentful. This only ended in more frustration. I was a victim, helpless against a hostile and sinful world. My only escape was the false sense of security I found in alcohol.

When I became involved with AA I was beaten. I surrendered to my alcoholism. I was taught that I could not change reality. This was better than always staring into the sun as I thought that was where the "fun" was. To change reality the AA Program taught me that I could change my perception of reality. A journal of my first year of recovery may have gone like this:

There are so many things that need changing. Why do I always have to be the one to change? Go to meetings and don't drink. Work the Steps. I hurt! It isn't worth it! Read the Big Book. Talk to my sponsor. How can they laugh! I'm really hurting! Go to meetings and don't drink. Work the Steps. One year dry. I have worked so hard is this all I get? Keep going to meetings. People are beginning to change. I begin to laugh with them. I begin to laugh at myself. I'm getting better. I cry. What a relief!

My recovery continues to progress with occasional lapses in my spiritual program. When I focus on my recovery, the world seems to be okay. I need to accept that I am always responsible for my own attitude and feelings—for my recovery itself. The more I accept this responsibility, the greater my freedom. I don't have to be controlled by outside forces. My perception of reality has changed and continues to change as a result of the Twelve Steps. I know that working the Steps to the best of my willingness results in a positive change for me and others. Step Twelve points out the results of working the first Eleven Steps—a spiritual awakening!

WILLINGNESS IS THE KEY
The Rewards Are Great

When I was in the throes of my worst drinking, I was living from day to day, sometimes hour to hour, in quiet desperation. It was only when I became **willing** to seek help for myself that I felt there might be some hope I might enjoy sobriety.

I stopped by the Club one day and talked with a lady, but that day I was only inquiring about AA for someone else. She immediately saw through the charade, but I did get some information. Not long after that I was ready and **willing** to do something about my drinking. I started attending three or four meetings a week, arriving just in time and leaving immediately after the meeting. Before long I changed this pattern, and when I acted friendly and not like a recluse, I got plenty of smiles and conversation. I could not talk at first—I could not bare my soul as I felt others were. But I finally became **willing** to talk at a meeting, and it was not nearly as difficult as I thought it might be. I think God realized I was finally **willing** to share my experience, and in return I received strength and more hope that the program really would work for me.

I did not consciously start to work the Twelve Steps, but I was fortunate in that I did listen and do as I was told by the real winners in the AA program, those who were living and **willing** to live the program daily.

It took more **willingness** to make an inventory of myself, to admit wrongs, to ask God to remove my defects of character, and to make amends to those I had hurt through my drinking. I have received the wonderful gift of sobriety (and I might add happy sobriety) some serenity, and a great deal of peace of mind through being **willing** to work this AA program each day of my life. I am **willing** to help other alcoholics. I must pass it on to keep it! If asked what one single thing in my life has meant the most and has been the most rewarding, I would answer, "Being sober through this God-given program of Alcoholics Anonymous." Thank God I was **willing** to listen, to learn, to practice the Twelve Steps. The reward has been great, and I feel most humble to have received this great gift of happy sobriety.[8]

II. SPIRITUALITY

SPIRITUAL HEALING
Let The Light Shine

More and more earnest people are talking about and turning to spiritual healing. The Founder of the Christian religion wrought wonders in making people whole. The faculty to relieve physical suffering was widespread in the early days of this era. The necessity of such a mission was enjoined on the followers of the Nazarene. But in later days the practice fell into disuse, probably because man became ever more preoccupied with subsistence and material things.

Today not only gifted clergymen, but physicians are gradually returning to the practice and with astounding results. Being men of science the doctors give it a mundane name: psychosomatic medicine. This means something that pertains to both the mind and the body.

In a less discerning time people drew a sharp line, a gulf of cleavage, between the physical and the spiritual. Today we see that they are facets of the same Power. Where, in a day of shattered atoms and the invasion of outer space does the scientific leave off and the spiritual begin? The same Force which created the material universe is the Power which placed that spark of divinity in man. It is all the same under different aspects.

From this approach the truth of the Biblical injunction that "as a man thinketh, so is he" becomes clear and meaningful.

Spiritual healing may be, then, just as scientific as medicine and medicine just as spiritual as one's faith will allow.

Overcoming the limitations of definitions which too often can immerse us in mental ruts, we should be aware that the greatest example of spiritual healing in modern times is the creation and growth of Alcoholics Anonymous.

Nowhere can a greater demonstration of the interlocking connection of the mental and the physical and the spiritual be found.

We believed in the omnipotence of a Higher Power and that the Higher Power made us whole again.

It is not necessary to go back to Bible stories to find accounts of healing miracles. There are hundreds of thousands of them in the membership of AA.

As mankind in these complex and tense days learns to return to the abiding Power which transcends all temporal affairs, they will come to look back on the founding of Alcoholics Anonymous as one of the most astounding pioneer developments in mankind's attempt to find itself.

The authors of the Twelve Steps were as inspired as any writer of old when, possibly with unconscious foresight, they talked about the need for a religious experience. This can come in many ways. It may not be sudden. It need not be denominational. But it must be a recognition of the unfailing source of Power that has in its keeping all the laws and manifestations of the universe whatever we call them.

Without the honest and desired application of what is now called spiritual healing none of us would have found this new life we enjoy. It has rid us of one of the worst diseases, one of the most complicated, that has afflicted mankind through the ages. It is complicated because it is mental and physical and because it wallows and battens in an absence of spiritual light. Once we let the light come in we are on the road to recovery; we have found a new world that anyone can enter if they believe.[4]

THE LORD'S PRAYER
As Related To The Twelve Steps

A friend of mine who just came into the program asked me recently how AA could claim to be a spiritual rather than a religious program when every meeting was closed with the Lord's Prayer—straight from the King James version of the Bible, and part of many Christian religious services. I didn't give her a very good answer at the time. I had asked this same question early in my sobriety, and had been told that there was a close relationship between the Steps of AA and the Lord's Prayer, and I had not thought about it further for some time. I decided to consider the question some more, and always being willing to rush in where angels (and theologians) fear to tread, I'll set down some of those thoughts later.

But first, it might be good to look back briefly on the earliest days of AA—the days before the fellowship was even called Alcoholics Anonymous. At that time, the "movement" was very much based on Protestant Christianity. At one time, some of the members of the movement felt that they should call themselves the "Jamesians" since many of their ideas for living sober were based on the New Testament writings of James. (Bill W. himself said that the first three Steps of AA were based in part on the Epistle of James.) The King James Bible and Christian religion were very much a part of the lives of those first persons who stayed sober. Many of them thought that it was necessary to have had some sort of grand revelation from above in order to achieve sobriety. In fact the early version of Step Twelve was: "Having had a spiritual experience..." rather than "Having had a spiritual awakening." Apparently it was not until Bill W. and many others formulated the ideas of what was to become the Big Book that it was fully clarified that AA really was for anyone and everyone who had a problem with alcohol, regardless of their religious, or lack of religious background. It was in writing the Steps for the purpose of the Big Book that the concept of "God" became the concept of "God, *as we understood Him*," and this is basic to AA's being spiritual rather than religious.

So we need not argue with the historical fact that AA was initially an outgrowth of Protestant Christianity. However, quite early on, wisdom, and I would even call it Divine wisdom, prevailed: AA actively renounced all religious sectarianism, and called itself strictly a spiritual program.

Now to my elaboration on my idea of how the AA Steps are related to the Lord's Prayer.

We begin, "Our Father, Who art in heaven." Step Two is related to this, in that we "Came to believe that (there is) a Power greater than ourselves..."

"Thy will be done on earth..." Step Three is related to this, in which we become willing to "turn our will . . . over to the care of God *as we understood Him*."

"Give us this day our daily bread." Again, this is Step Three, where we are willing to turn our lives over to the care of God. A little more explanation: The prayer does not say "Show us how to earn our daily bread," it says that we are, in fact, putting our trust in God that He will provide for us—turning our lives over to His care.

"Forgive us our trespasses, as we forgive those who trespass against us." This is a biggie! The way in which we carry this out is in Steps Four through Ten. In these Steps we identify our own trespasses as well as what we perceive as trespasses against us, and we do something about all of them. In this process we relive our own conscience (forgive us our trespasses), and we unload our past resentments (as we forgive those who trespass against us).

"Lead us not into temptation, but deliver us from evil." It may not be stretching a point too fine to relate this to part of Steps Eleven and Twelve: "praying only for knowledge of His will for us and the power to carry that out," and "tried . . . to practice these principles in all our affairs."

Finally, again we have a reaffirmation of our faith in a power greater than ourselves, Step Two, in "For Thine is the kingdom, and the power, and the glory forever."[9]

FINDING ADVICE IN THE
DARNDEST PLACES
The Sermon On The Mount

The other day, curiosity caused me to read the report of the Sermon on the Mount by Matthew in the New Testament.

And once again I was reminded that the things we are told in AA to do in order to make our sobriety serene and spiritual growth possible always work because they have been serving mankind for some 2,000 years.

Of course, AA is not a religious program (I personally stopped church going at 20), but when we heed the advice not to project and to live only one day at a time, we are attending to some things their Teacher told the twelve disciples. He said: "Do not be anxious about tomorrow, for tomorrow will be anxious for itself," and "let the day's own troubles be sufficient for the day."

How familiar today is the encouragement to "Pray for the SOB." Words spoken on the Mount were, "Pray for those who treat you badly."

Daily in AA we hear that our program is for those who want it. Not far from the words, "Knock and the door will open for you . . . He who searches shall find."

Self-pitiers are told in AA today to get off the pity pot. What I read in Matthew was "Do not put on a gloomy look so that all men shall know you are fasting (hurting)."

We quote the advice to do good deeds without anyone but ourselves ever knowing about them. We can find that the apostles were told, "Do not do your good deeds in public in order to be seen by others . . . so that your charity may be secret."

We give in AA without expectations of receiving. Christ preached, "Lend to those who need, hoping for nothing in return."

In AA, we carry the message for no other reason than self-satisfaction. In Christ's sermon, we find, "If you do good only to those who do good to you, why expect a reward? If you lend to those from whom you expect to receive, why think that you deserve thanks?"

It was surprising to find in that ages-old sermon a counter-part to our "Keep it simple." Christ said, "Let what you say be simple."

And perhaps this quote from the sermon rings a modern AA bell: "If you forgive others what they do wrong, you will . . . forgive you."[9]

A RATIONAL SPIRITUAL EXPERIENCE
Self-Control By Ideals

The spiritual phase of AA to me, is a conscious experience. Not necessarily an elaborate or striking affair, but a sincere desire to know, to feel, to grow in a conscious scope and power toward sobriety.

It comes when an alcoholic, of their own choice, consciously change their Way of Life, to a noble choice of spiritual ideals.

A nourishing change of heart, to a new Way of Life, the AA way.

There, you see, is a spiritual experience, a new ability, new might, seeking from a Power greater than yourself the help that you need to carry on this new Way of Life. It changes weak and dispirited consciousness into strong, energetic will.

It is not enough to say that spirit is a conscious experience. It must be a noble emotion, directed toward the up-building of character as a whole in yourself and others.

Its nobility lies in its scope, its rationality, its unselfishness, and its devotion to ideals. It is a movement of the mind away from the lower levels to higher ideals which will fit into our new personality.

It is not necessarily spiritual if it be regarded merely as one more interest and leaves worldly habits unchanged. It may have to be mechanical at first. It does not become spiritual until it actually enobles our life, and relates it to the Plan and Purposes of the AA Way of Life.

Nothing is more of a travesty on the Spiritual Power of AA, than a meager, poverty-stricken attitude, which is hardly more than a symbol. It must be sufficient, adequate, and must help us to discover the possibilities of the AA plan and help us to live up to the ideals for which it was formed.

A Rational Spiritual Experience means being consistent and normal in our behavior.

Neither Faith nor Emotion need be unreasonable. Being irrational is being deliberately exclusive. It closes our eyes and hearts to facts and truth, and is inconsistent.

From this definition, it is clear that the Spiritual Phase of AA is rational, inclusive, consistent, and orderly.

It is a principle of self-control by ideals. Spirit, then, is Power, Inspiration, Freedom, and can be identified by its conformity to Ideals of Goodness, Faith, Honesty, Reverence, and to our Four Absolutes.[31]

Note: **THE FOUR ABSOLUTES**
1.   Absolute Honesty
2.   Absolute Purity
3.   Absolute Unselfishness
4.   Absolute Love

SPIRITUAL MILESTONES IN ALCOHOLICS ANONYMOUS
Seven Suggestions

Few, if any, men or women have completely fulfilled the aims of Alcoholics Anonymous without at least some grasp of the **spiritual**. True, there have been some who have managed to keep sober simply by mechanical action. But a preponderance of evidence points out that until one has some spiritual conviction, and the more the better, they take no joy in their sobriety. Too often we hear an AA remark, "I think this is a wonderful program, but I can't understand the spiritual angle." To them the "religion" otherwise known as Alcoholics Anonymous is something too complex, abstract, and awesome. They seem to have the impression that "religion," the spiritual life, is something to be enjoyed only by saints, the clergy, and perhaps an occasional highly privileged layman. They cannot conceive that it can be for the reformed "sinner" as well. And yet the truth is, the spiritual program of AA is there for all of us to enjoy.

But, ask the alcoholic, where can I find a simple, step-by-step "religious" guide? The Ten Commandments give us a set of Thou Shalts and Thou Shalt Nots; the Twelve Steps of AA give us a program of dynamic action; but what about a spiritual guide?

Of course the answer is that by following the Ten Commandments and Twelve Steps to the letter we automatically lead a spiritual life, whether or not we recognize it.

Here, however, is a set of suggestions stated in the simplest of language:

1. Eliminate sin from our lives.
2. Develop humility.
3. Constantly pray to God for guidance.
4. Practice charity.
5. Meditate frequently on our new-found blessings, giving honest thanks to them.
6. Take God into our confidence in all our acts.
7. Seek the companionship of others who are seeking a spiritual life.

These are practical suggestions, milestones on the road to a spiritual life. There is nothing mysterious about them. Every one of the seven points is found elsewhere in AA literature, but here they are set down in a group for easier guidance. Let's look at each point briefly:

1. *Eliminate sin from our lives.*

We take a long step toward the spiritual life when we do a bit of personal housecleaning. It is utterly essential, if we are to retain sobriety, to eliminate the imperfections of lust, greed, selfishness, intolerance, gluttony, sloth, anger, jealousy—to mention a few. Most of all we must banish the twin devils of an alcoholic, self-pity and resentment. A non-alcoholic may be able to indulge occasionally in some of these sins without great harm or a complete moral setback resulting. But for an alcoholic such indulgence can be fatal.

2. *Develop humility.*

This is of a more abstract nature than the other points, hard to pin down. The simplest example, perhaps, is this: When you hear an AA say, "I can't understand the spiritual angle of the program," note that it is almost invariably said wistfully. In other words, they would **like to understand** the spiritual program. For humility is teachability, the willingness to learn, keeping an open mind. An inner feeling of unworthiness is healthy in the sight of God.

3. *Constantly pray to God for guidance.*

Prayer is a partnership. A foreman in a great corporation can get an idea that will benefit his company. But before the plan can be accepted it must go before the board of directors, men of wisdom and experience. And after it is accepted it is the foreman and men working with him who must put it into effect. In our personal lives God is the elder statesman. We ask Him for guidance, but we must do the work. It is logical to believe that if every person in the world prayed sincerely for peace, peace would be forthcoming. But every person would have to do their part. We cannot pray for something that is apparently out of our reach, then sit back and expect God to dump it in our laps. But if we pray sincerely, then do our part by taking dynamic action, even things we thought beyond attainment will fall like a ripe plum.

4. *Practice charity.*

This is simply another way of saying practice the Twelfth Step. The unselfish helping of others is the practice of love. Remember, "What is hateful to thee, do not unto thy fellow man; this is the whole Law; the rest is mere commentary."

5. *Meditate frequently on our newly found blessings, giving honest thanks for them.*

This is self-evident, and, if one posesses the least spark of gratitude for his sobriety, is spontaneous. We who have known the very depth of despair are more likely to be grateful for the little blessings of life, such as freedom from fear and worries, love of our families and friends, respect from others and self-respect, than those non-alcoholics who take such things for granted. We have ample reason for gratitude. Our blessings are proof that there is a God who will guide and bless us as long as we do our part.

6.   *Take God into our confidence in all our acts.*

In other words, ponder the rightness or wrongness of every thought, word, or action. One of the chief blessings of being an adult is to be able to distinguish between right and wrong. Regardless of how profitable an idea may seem, if conscience tells us it is unethical, disregard it. We should always strive to make God a companion rather than someone from whom we constantly demand gifts.

7.   *Seek the companionship of others who are seeking the spiritual life.*

In the early days, the kitchen was the "church" of Alcoholics Anonymous. The few members met almost every morning to have coffee together, pray together, and give thought to their mutual problems. AA was a shaky structure in those days, with but a few members, no literature except the Bible, no rules for guidance except a few inherited from the Oxford Group. They had to depend on fellowship, even more than we do today. AA has been described by medicine as group therapy. The successful AA program of today is an accumulation of knowledge and ideas arrived at by trial and error of not only those early members, but of hundreds of thousands who have contributed even up to this very day. Although, for example, the Twelve Steps may have been composed by one man, they are actually the result of mass thinking. The author wrote them after absorbing and sorting out the various thoughts gained in association and conversation with other alcoholics. Who can say who first discovered one of the very cornerstones of AA, the 24-Hour Plan? Who can say who first applied the phrase "Easy Does It" to our program? One of your own ideas, publicly spoken, may within a year or two be accepted as a tenet of AA. Alcoholics Anonymous are **your** people. You are safe in their company. Your mastery of the sober life will grow in proportion to the contact you have with your AA friends. Not only do we attain stature by attending AA meetings, but by meeting our new friends for lunch, sitting with them on the front porch in summertime, dropping by to see them in the evening. The conversation will turn to our common problems, to the benefit of all.

Some of us find God in unusual and unexpected ways. Some are fortunate to have a sudden illuminating experience that changes their lives within a space of minutes. The majority have the experience more slowly, a gradual growth over a number of years. The ultimate aim of all men is peace of spirit. Without a spiritual life there can be no tranquility and serenity. We will find peace when our lives are rightly ordered.

There can be no better safeguard to sobriety than faith and trust in God. It can be cultivated through prayer and observing the happiness of those who live a blameless life.

Alcoholics have more of a task in attaining a state of grace than normal persons. Spiritual growth has been slow but progressive in most non-alcoholics. They were introduced to religion in childhood and for the most part have advanced year by year. Alcoholics, too, were introduced to religion early in life, but abandoned it for many years during their drinking careers.

Spiritual laws are as immutable as the laws of mathematics. As certainly as two plus two equals four, so does evil beget evil and good beget good.

The ways of God are mysterious, but don't we meet mystery constantly in daily life? The worker in the airplane factory is given a small blueprint that doesn't seem to make much sense of itself. He follows that blueprint because he knows the the man upstairs has the master plan. So the Man Upstairs gives us a small section of the blueprint of Life. We follow it and our lives become an orderly segment of the Universe.

The power of God has been likened to the electric power line that runs by our homes. We can fill the home with the finest appliances, but until we plug into the electric power line they will not run. So are our lives unsatisfactory until we plug into the Power of God.

The Twelve Steps are a steep, hard climb. But as we make the climb we can make it easier by remembering there are two handrails—God and AA.[10]

HE WORKS IN MYSTERIOUS WAYS
God's Guidance

No doubt many of us have heard some speaker or individual member say, "I came into AA just to get my wife off my back, but after attending meetings with some regularity and staying in dry places, I decided that this is what I wanted."

Undoubtedly, there are many men and women who found sobriety through this fellowship, who have never paused to let their minds run back to the chain of events which brought our fellowship up to its present status, or to the events which brought them into AA, where they found the very thing they were looking for. We cannot find an adequate explanation that it was only by chance that an alcoholic from New York came to Akron, Ohio and found a church directory in a hotel lobby which got him in touch with another alcoholic in Akron and together they formed a world-wide fellowship to help all alcoholics, who want and need help. Is it only a coincidence that today there are thousands of AA groups throughout the world and about a million alcoholics who found sobriety through this fellowship which these two men formed?

God works in mysterious ways and it is beyond the human mind to fully understand how a blind chance can shuffle and mold from it the right men and women at the right time, for the right purpose. To know God's work and His love for man by reason alone is not enough. Just as it is impossible to know courage, love, and sympathy merely by reading the definition of them. The real knowing requires personal experience.

Surely, it was not just coincidence that brought the man into AA just to get his wife off his back. No doubt there was a combination of events which caused him to want what he saw. Such as attending the example of others and most importantly, the prayers of some loved one. God's guidance comes in various ways and there are many men and women sober today, who came into AA by different routes. Some to get their wife and their boss off their back, or to get into good grace with the family, but the prayer of a loved one was what made them face reality and follow God's direction.

We, who have found sobriety through this fellowship, should never forget that God selected us from among millions of alcoholics and our value to our fellowship will be determined by our gratitude and by the way we follow God's direction. The road which God points out to us may not be an easy one and it may involve some pain and sacrifice. We don't know what lies ahead but definitely we know that those who follow God's guidance will grow in character. Whatever we think of our founders and the men and women who believed that there is a Higher Power presiding over the world, they were convinced that God rules the affairs of man and they were certain if they follow His direction they would never fail, and as a result of their faith, the Fellowship of Alcoholics Anonymous has spread across the world.

Looking back over the years and the progress of Alcoholics Anonymous up to this point, we cannot say that all those events which made AA strong came about coincidentally. Alcoholics Anonymous was built on a spiritual foundation with the bricks of love and service by men and women who faithfully followed God's instructions. They translated love and service into action and established a true understanding between God and man.[16]

AN AA MEETING
Miracles Do Happen

"Alcoholics Anonymous is an informal society of alcoholics who aim to help fellow drinkers recover their health" . . . the chairman for the evening is reading "The Purpose of This AA Meeting." There are 15, maybe 20 members in the room tonight. A new man who hasn't had a drink in almost eight hours—eternity—shifts uncomfortably in his chair. His thinking is foggy . . . he's coming off a long binge . . . a series of long binges stretching back over 20 years.

The chairman is still reading, but the new man doesn't hear much: "We know that many of our number have already laid the foundation for permanent recovery in spite of the fact that we have often been pronounced incurable. We alcoholics are gathered together seeking a renewal of strength. This strength has been revealed to us as coming from a power higher than an earthly one . . . ."

The new man tries to see the wristwatch on the member next to him . . . it looks like two minutes after eight . . . How's he going to sit here an hour? He eyes the distance to the door and fidgets nervously. The member offers him a cigarette. He's almost too shaky to take it . . . reaching for it makes him shake more. He wants to run . . . to get the hell out. The member helps him with the cigarette, helps him light it; the smoke helps him a little. The chairman is still reading: "Not being reformers, we offer our help and experience only to those who want it. The only requirement for membership is an honest willingness to do anything to stop drinking . . . . Each person present is requested to observe the exact meaning of the word anonymous as many of our members wish to remain anonymous."

Then with an extemporaneous remark or two, the chairman introduces the first speaker, a businessman from another city who just happens to be in Nashville. A tall, gray-haired man leaves his seat in the third row and walks to the front. When he faces the group you can see the character, the friendliness in his face . . . a couple of scars, too, if you look closely. He must be 55, give or take a year or two. His clothes are well-tailored; he stands erect; he's a fine looking man.

But in the jaundiced eye of the new man, "He's some big shot . . . got his, then got religion . . . now he wants to lecture somebody. I've got to have a drink, not a sermon . . . I can't stand this," he thinks.

The gray-haired man starts talking. "My name is Mack _____. I am an alcoholic. By the grace of God and the help of Alcoholics Anonymous I am sober tonight, and will be sober for the next 24 hours." His voice is soft and clear. He's not a "speech-maker," he's just talking . . . sincerely.

"Haven't thought over anything to talk about, didn't know I'd be called on tonight. But I'll tell you a little story.

"Five years ago, in -------, Texas, a battered, beaten, derelict drunk crawled behind a signboard in a vacant lot. This man—if you'd call him a man—was barefoot. His clothing consisted of a ragged shirt and ragged pants . . . that's all. Both garments were filthy . . . and stinking. He was clutching a two-bit bottle of wine, about half full. He was wild-eyed and shaking hard all over. He went into screaming DTs back of that signboard, and the cops found him. They had to fight for his empty bottle. They had to have help to put him in a padded cell. They had to have a doctor quiet him. His terrified shrieks kept the whole jail on edge for hours.

"When he was able the following Monday to appear before the judge, he got this lecture: 'I've been on this bench for 13 years, and for 13 years you've been coming before me. Drunk charge. You've never, to my knowledge, in all those 13 years made even a pretense at working. How you've lived, God only knows. I've tried to help you . . . hospital, asylum. I've tried by punishment—workhouse, county road. You always come back in the same condition—drunk! The most worthless, disgraceful human—I presume you're human—I've ever seen. You're a disgrace to this city and I'm at my wit's end. I instruct these officers to take you to the city limits, start you out and see that you don't come back. Now get out . . . and stay out.'

"As the police left the City Hall with this human wreck they were accosted by two men. Nice looking men. Alcoholics Anonymous, they said. The officers gave them the story, let them question the prisoner. 'Do you want to quit drinking? Really want to quit drinking?' The old man looked at them. His bleary eyes expressed his suffering. 'Do I want to quit? Good God, man, are you crazy? But there isn't any way to quit. I'll die drunk, I know it. The sooner the better.' Would he be willing to try another hospital? A hesitant yes. Would the judge let them try? Well . . . yes, but only on condition.

"With three weeks of nursing by those two AAs and a couple of others, the 'old boy' began to look almost human. They cleaned him up. They helped him get a job. They helped him mostly 'spiritually,' when the going was rough, when he needed help the most. When he needed a drink—badly—they helped him stay sober. And then he began to get a grip, he caught on, he became a different man. He was born . . . in an AA club . . . just like this. He's still sober too. He's still grateful, and he still makes AA meetings . . . regularly! And every once in a while, whenever he's given the privilege, that man gives another drunk a hand. You know who that man is? That man is me."

There are other speakers, too, who have stories, their own stories, different stories . . . yet the same.

Sometime during the meeting tonight the new man has gotten a faint glimmer of something. Maybe it's hope. Maybe it's friendship. Maybe it's understanding. These people, or maybe some of them, have been through the same . . . his mind is still foggy. The meeting is closing, the group is repeating the Lord's Prayer, they seem to be emphasizing, just a little, "Thy will be done" . . . "give us this day" . . . "as we forgive." The new man wants to talk to somebody, to the gray-haired speaker. They have coffee and others join them. They talk, talk the same language, talk late. He feels at home; he feels friendship; he needs it . . . desperately.

And this is the story of an AA meeting which was held September, 1946, in the old clubhouse on Fifth Avenue. The new man is still sober . . . and well remembers how he felt . . . for that night five and a half years ago, I, the writer, was the new man.

MY REFLECTIONS ON THE THIRD STEP
As A Newcomer And At 7 & 14 Years Sobriety

One night during my fifth year of sobriety my sixteen-year-old son was critically hurt in a railroad right-of-way accident and in a few hours he died. My daughter asked me, "Didn't you pray?" I told her I had. She said, "Then why did he die?"

I'm glad I had had several years experience in trying to work the third of AA's suggested Twelve Steps: "Made a decision to turn our will and our lives over to the care of God *as we understood Him*," before I was called upon to answer that one.

My daughter's question, I think, throws out a fundamental challenge to all of us who would like to live the life proposed by the Twelve Steps and to grow in it year by year.

What she had really asked was: "Since you are such good friends with God, and since He is almighty, why doesn't He perform this simple, for Him, act of healing when you ask Him to?" For several years I had let her know I was trying to give God a greater share in my life, and that He had taken over and solved many of my most pressing problems. She had concluded that the old man had made connections Up There and could pull wires when there was a real pinch.

There is more to this, I contend, than a child's over-confidence in a parent. She has tossed us one of the fundamental questions for beginners in the spiritual life, which might be phrased somewhat as follows: "Does conscious contact with the Higher Power improve with time?"

The external evidence seems to be inconclusive. When I think of a certain officially consecrated man of the cloth whose home people will change their route to avoid passing, and of a certain veteran of sobriety I dare not trust with a confidence, I say "no." When I think of another clergyman whose presence always means peace, and of a certain old-timer whose mere handshake is a tonic, I say "yes." Clearly, the mere passage of time since first acknowledgment of a greater Power is not the governing factor. What we really ask, I suppose, is whether contact improves for those who sincerely want it to.

Here we enter the world of the subjective, the deeply personal. Am I sincere? Only I can say. To my friends I may appear as phony as a Brooklyn gondolier, but if I know in my heart that I'm doing my level best, however poor that may look to outsiders, they're wrong. Or my group associates may consider me very much on the beam, but if inwardly I know they're misled by my unctuous delivery of pat formulae, they're wrong again. Only I (and the Higher Power) can know I'm really in earnest. So we recast the query into this form: "Does conscious contact with God improve with time for those who in their deepest hearts sincerely want it to?"

For many of us who have "been in" for a time, this is an important question. Anyway, it's an important question for me, (now aboard nearly seven years), and for some of my friends of comparable seniority. Sometimes we suspect, perhaps a little moodily, that we're not getting anywhere? We need a freshener, a perker-upper, a checkup, a spiritual eye-opener, perhaps a goose. How shall we get it?

One good way, I have found, is to go back to Step Three and review it carefully, and ask ourselves what it once meant to us, and what our accumulated experience with it has been, and what it means to us right now, in this instant: "Made a decision to turn our will and our lives over the care of God *as we understood Him.*"

What does this mean to you?

This is what it means to me:

During my first few weeks in AA I stayed sober on excitement, preoccupation with a novelty, and the busyness of reading, going to meetings, and absorbing the mechanics of daily sobriety. From my first reading of the Twelve Steps I recognized the Third to be pivotal, and kept a sharp ear cocked for tips on how it might be managed. "I just let go and let God," I heard people say. Or, "I saw I could do nothing so I just turned it over," or, "I can't handle it, God. You take over."

They "just" handed things over! Just! If only it could be so simple for me! I longed to be rid of my burdens, and sought everywhere for the Higher Power upon whom I could dump them. Where was He to be found? On what terms did the transaction take place? When you wanted to surrender, who accepted your ceremonial sword, and in what setting? For months these questions hammered through my thinking, and nobody seemed to have any but the vaguest answers.

It was critical time for me, I now realize. My sobriety was at stake. This program had encouraged me to look forward to a glorious relationship with the Creator of the Universe Himself, an eternal friendly collaboration that would leap all obstacles and transcend all defeats. I was to walk hand in hand with God, they had said. All right, I responded, here I am. Where is God? For weeks and weeks I waited. He had accepted the surrender of many others. Could it be that He would not accept mine?

One day it happened. I was really at the end of my rope, or to mix a figure, they had me properly hemmed in. My (then) family had just been broken past mending. I was broke. My business connections no longer existed. My only hope had been work in progress; this depended on good morale and a clear head, and these assets had taken flight. Everywhere I looked, futility stared back at me.

This was frustration beyond the kind that gets people drunk; I had learned that getting drunk wouldn't fix it. It was despair, all the worse because it was sober despair. Then, all at once, the actual phraseology of the Step Three came bright and clear to my mind. Particularly, as if neon-lighted, the first words stood out: "Made a decision."

It occurred to me that all these weeks I'd been trying to surrender, when the step asked nothing of the kind. It only suggested I make a decision to do so. I surveyed my situation and asked myself if I really wanted to take such a step. When I decided I really did, I issued a kind of proclamation. I don't remember verbalizing it, but if I had, it would have been something like this: "Surrendering will and life means giving up the right to make decisions concerning them. I therefore proclaim that from this moment until better advised I will make no decision concerning my own actions, that I will follow only unpremeditated whims. These I declare arbitrarily to be the will of God for me; except when obviously harmful I will obey them without question."

As I read this over I find myself praying that no one will take my seemingly preposterous course as reasonable for another. In retelling it I am not claiming what was good for me is good for others—only that whatever is specifically good for a person will come to him if he will endure, with the best faith he can muster, to what seems the very extremity. For me, my odd renunciation of decision led to my first really vivid spiritual experience.

How do I know whether I'm having a spiritual experience or just kidding myself? For many months after my adventure, this question bothered me. Whenever someone spoke of having a spiritual experience I questioned him closely on its nature; in my reading I searched for clues. In my own case there were no visions or alternations of natural surroundings.

Then how do I know it was really spiritual? Two ways: I felt a mighty reassurance come upon me from a source outside myself. My conviction that man has access to the loving, caring Creator of the Universe was permanently deepened.

These two qualities seem common to all the spiritual experiences I've ever heard or read about, regardless of what else may have happened. What matters is the feeling, during or immediately after the experience itself, that says: "This must be the touch of the Higher Power I've been hearing about!" These feelings can arrive through the most unlikely channels at the most improbable times, or they can descend precisely according to ecclesiastical formula. They can come through the touch of a friend or the look of a total stranger; they can leap from a printed page or emerge from a blank wall; they can be intense or mild. After comparing notes I've concluded tentatively that the only common denominator is a feeling of reassurance.

Once a person has become convinced that he has established contact, if only momentarily, with the Higher Power, how does he maintain and reinforce that contact? This, to me, is the toughest aspect of Step Three.

For years I have sought to make an assured part of my daily experience the wonderful sense of harmony I knew in the interval of my first spiritual experience. I have failed. Having failed, I am forced to one of two conclusions. One is that God does not want me to have that sense of harmony with him as a permanent possession. This alternative I do not accept. I am therefore forced to the other: He is trying to teach me some lesson that must be learned before the desired relationship can become permanent.

What could this lesson be? Sometimes, in some moods, I have an inkling. He is trying to show me He is God, and I am only I.

Why should this simple lesson be so hard? I have no answer to that one; I only report that it is. I'm always trying to get God to run errands for me and do chores it would be convenient for me to have done. He always stands on His prerogative. He is God, and He does as He pleases Being God, He runs no man's errands, does no man's chores, save when He pleases.

He may please not to be a chore-boy—and this, to the temperament of which many alcoholics and many, many others are made is unforgivable. God is supposed to carry out our orders; when He declines to do so, we get mad at Him. I am convinced that much of the attitude of man that passes as disbelief in God is in reality only rage against Him for not behaving as individuals want Him to. My daughter said, "Then why did he die? Didn't my Dad tell God what was expected of Him? Then why didn't He do it?" What does He mean, always insisting on doing this His own way? Who does He think He is—God?

That, of course, is exactly who He thinks He is. Whenever I have found the means to let Him go ahead and be the God of my universe I have never regretted it. When His ways of doing things seem too unendurably contrary to my own, he often takes the trouble to explain to me, through some new and always unexpected enlightenment, the advantages of His way. Thus have I been able to survive frequent denials of my will and still maintain at least an intention of allegiance to Him. Thus, incidentally, has my young and non-alcoholic daughter also been guided to continue her trust in Him. Here I have to say a word about getting sore at God. On the very morning of the day on which I write these words of allegiance, I was angry at God. When my son died I was angry at God for a time because I thought He had been unfair to me. When I'm broke, or unjustly accused, or when I work long and faithfully without reward, I often accuse God of having deserted me and I get sore.

For a long time I was afraid to admit anger to God. When I was a boy, to question my father's judgement angrily was to invite a beating; my experience with employers has led me to conclude that bringing the bosses' decision to ill-tempered account invites devastating retaliation. Suppose God, with his inestimable power, should get mad at me! Instead, He seems more often to teach me, when I'm willing to be taught. I frequently have it out with him, saying, "God, this seems to me an outrageous deal, I'm surprised and disappointed and mad that You'd allow it!"

Sometimes He seems to admit it's outrageous, and suggests I put up with it anyhow, for the sake of some objective He sees to be worthwhile in the long run. Other times He convinces me that it wasn't so outrageous as I had supposed. That He'll condescend to explain to the likes of me is what C.S. Lewis once called "the intolerable compliment of loving us." That He does love us is now to me beyond question. This makes it much easier for me, as an older member, to turn my will and my life over to Him as often as seems necessary—that is to say, daily. For I am an alcoholic, and I can't afford to let my speculations wander too far beyond the immediate considerations of this day.

Seven Years After That—

For a time during World War II, I was privileged to live in England while it was being bombed, and see how valiantly a nation can rally to an emergency. After the war, my British friends tell me, there was a lapse from these high standards of courtesy, generosity, and courage. Not everybody, but most people tended to retreat to the old bog of rancor, indifference, and selfishness.

Sometimes I wonder whether something similar may not happen in AA. Certainly there has been a tendency toward it in my own case. During the critical battle with my deadly enemy alcohol, I was ready to go all the way with good to overcome this single evil. No sacrifice of time, property, or status was too great for the prize of sobriety. I came to Step Three. Turn my will and my life over to the care of God? Gladly and without reservation—here it is.

Now, after a sequence of twenty-four-hour periods carrying me into my fourteenth year, I'm getting an inkling of what Step Three may mean over the long haul. The enemy that had been a fire-breathing dragon squarely blocking the main highway, now takes the form of a small, venomous snake slithering through the weeds in the byways.

Some of the tumult and shouting has died. The struggle has entered a quieter, inward phase, subtler, possibly less exciting, but I think more profound.

Shouldn't persons as well as nations gird, not just for the crisis, but for the long pull from here in? Fourteen years ago, when I entered AA—even seven years ago when I was writing for these pages an "older member's" comments on Step Three—

it seemed to me that the "decision" called for was in the nature of an outgoing, almost aggressive act. I was supposed to find God and give Him—thrust upon Him, if necessary—something He didn't have and possibly didn't want.

As I understand it now, our wills and our lives are already in the care of God. In Step Three we only stop fighting an existing fact—the one really decisive circumstance of our entire existence—and consciously acknowledge what already is.

Playing in a tree near my house is a gray squirrel who, I am almost sure, hasn't the least awareness of the fact that his will and life are in the care of God. Nevertheless they are—he can will nothing of life not provided for by nature, a creative force which springs, I confidently believe, from God. Aside from some anatomical details, the big difference between the squirrel and me is that I can become aware of this relationship with God and the squirrel cannot.

Does this awareness change anything? I think it does. If I know my will and life are bounded by God's creation and hence His care, and do nothing about it, I'm but little ahead of the squirrel. If, however, I try to find out what God is interested in and make friends with Him, there's no telling what I may someday become—certainly something better than I now am.

At this point I can hear some of my keep-it-simple friends asking, justifiably, what this has to do with keeping sober. It has this to do with it: I'm pretty sure that if the AA program didn't offer me a continuing chance to grow, I'd soon be drunk. We are not saints, but I'm not short of human frailty, and have room for vast improvement without seeming to buck for sainthood. In AA you grow or shrink; I, if I can, would like to grow, both in understanding and in capacity to help.

Of course, knowledge that our lives and wills are totally enclosed in God's creation, doesn't mean we have to play along with Him. The universe is set up to allow for quite a lot of rebellion. However, as I come to know Him a little, He seems gentle and good as well as mighty and sometimes stern. I no longer want to rebel. I'd prefer to find out what He's interested in, if possible, and get interested in these same things myself. We might then be closer than we are now, and I'd like that.

He is interested, I think, in developing better people. I say this, of course, with no inside track or special authorization; just from reading about Him and watching how He seems to be working in AA and other areas, and respecting my own hunch. Evolution always starts with something in existence, then improves on it. It's my surmise that whenever we're helping someone, including ourselves, to be a better person, we're doing something God is interested in. Our will and our lives are then not only in His hands, but are harmonious with His will and life, realizing the full meaning and purpose of our creation.

For a long time, it bothered me that the times of vivid awareness that my will and life are really in God's care, were brief and far apart. Lately, I'm less concerned about that. I, like the squirrel, have nuts to gather—human things to do requiring such concentration that I am unaware of God, even though in the midst of Him and doing tasks He has assigned me. When the job is done, though, as Step Three puts it, I make a decision.

"Made a decision"—a more complicated business than I ever imagined! Once, in my frustrated pre-AA efforts to make sense of life, I got psychoanalyzed and learned something about my mental machinery. Besides an often perverse ego and some conflicting unconscious drives, I have a carping superego that bedevils every decision I try to make—arguing, negating, scolding. Nevertheless, doing my best with what I've got, I decide to turn my will and my life over to the care of God—and this, to me, is the same as realizing my life and will are already in His care.

In striving for this awareness, it helped me to remember some things about my own relation to the universe, and to other people—that there are nearly three thousand generations, that the earth is big, that the sun is ninety-three million miles away, that the Milky Way is two hundred light years across, that it's only one little galaxy among billions, that somehow I'm a part of a magnificent, continuing, creative stream. Slowly, the grandeur of Him, to whom my will and life are entrusted, begins to come through.[11]

SURRENDER
We Had To Quit Playing God

Man, like the bee and the ant, is a purely social creature so that the value of the individual lies solely in the value of his contribution to the common good, which is the sum total of his contributions to his family, his friends, and his community. But man, being a creature of logic, demands that even his bit part in the tremendous drama of life should have a few lines in the manuscript, and that the whole production should make sense. The quandary of modern man lies in his failure to edit and assimilate the upheaval of the current social, scientific, and industrial revolutions into anything more coherent than a delirious *Alice in Wonderland* stage production. Ancient man felt secure living as a contented subject when he believed firmly in the divine right of his King, while modern man winds up under comedy characters like Franco, Stalin, or some of our Washington crop. Ancient man lived placidly under an accepted official community religion, while modern man spins in a vortex of science, sects, cults, doubt, and confusion. It is small wonder that so many of us say, "To hell with it," and throw away our scrambled lines to write our own script and stage our own production.

It is significant of our time that the tragic Henley who wrote so bravely, "I am the Captain of my fate, I am the Master of my Soul," put a bullet through his brilliant brain. We alcoholics have all played at being Invictus, with heads bloody but unbowed. It is again significant that we only succeed when we bow our bloodied heads in simple prayer, and sheath our blunted swords to end our furious battle of the windmills in the gin mills.

It is the firm belief of many of us that no man ever fails in AA who has completed our Third Step; who has turned his will and his life over to the care of God as he understands him. If you examine this critical step to see why we seem to lose it, other than the psychological fact that the human mind is geared to forget unpleasant things first. During the early years AA was a part of the Oxford Group to whom Surrender was the key step that the neophyte took in entering their fellowship, a step accompanied by reverent ceremony. But it is most difficult and distasteful for an egocentric alcoholic to give up his gold braid as self-appointed arbiter of the Universe so we have de-emphasized, and even forgotten "surrender" in the ensuing years. According to their literature, the Oxford Group's initial act of surrender is a simple decision put into simple language spoken aloud to God in front of witnesses, that we have decided to forget the past in God and to give our future into His keeping. Nothing more need be added, nothing can be taken away!

Their reasoning concerning this key step was expressed by Harold Begbie in his book, *Life Changer*, and can be summarized:

> No man can sound the depths of his own natural peace nor rise to the heights of his own natural bliss who is not conscious of the presence and the companionship of God. Consciousness of God is the natural state of things. Sin is unnatural in the sense that it is the will of the creature opposing the will of the Creator.
>
> It is a word which denotes a choosing; the will chooses the bad, while it is its duty, in the interest of the world, to choose the good. It is fatal to its own peace to choose the bad, but it does choose the bad. The act of choosing constitutes the sin. All sin is an attempt on the part of the human will to reverse the process of growth, to descend instead of ascend. The will which chooses the bad therefore is in opposition to the will of the

universe, that is to say, the will of God. Realization of the divine companionship depends solely and exclusively on one act of the will, an act which denies the animal senses and embraces with an absolute and unquestioning surrender, the will of our Creator."

It may be wise to retrace our earlier path and quit the mass production shilling of lushes out of barrooms and into AA "coke-tail" lounges and poker clubs. We can attempt a little quality control on our therapy by returning to our earlier methods. We should sharply distinguish the disease from the cure, and evaluate our actions to discern whether what we do is a part of the disease, or part of the cure.

Dr. Tiebout said: "Characteristic of the typical alcoholic is a narcissistic egocentric core, dominated by feelings of omnipotence, and intent on maintaining at all costs its inner integrity." Dr. Stillman, in addition, noted "defiant individuality and grandiosity" as group characteristics of problem drinkers. Alcoholics Anonymous has convincingly demonstrated that a spiritual group therapy can remove these character defects, to make possible the rebuilding of a shattered life; but only when the jug has beaten the toper into an unconditional surrender of that egocentric core. By abandoning the unconditional surrender as a requirement for AA membership we have increased our numbers, but not our quality, having opened the doors to any jug-head wishing to get the heat off at home or at the office. We have also introduced the strange phenomenon of the "dry drunkard" into our ranks. This interesting would-be monarch of all he surveys, remains completely unsurrendered and incorrigible, and can baffle and bewilder any discussion meeting to a degree seldom found this side of Washington.

We gradually observe in our fellowship that it is our

stinking pride and bleeding ego that alone prevents the acceptance of our spiritual therapy, that causes us to slip, and which if not abandoned, will drag us to the gutter or the grave. We learn that we were just little Caesars, proclaiming ourselves both God and Emperor, with the bar our holy shrine and altar. But our real knowledge begins when a true objective viewpoint shows us what a lousy tin god our ego has made us, and what vile shrines we had erected with our bottles. It is then that the unconditional surrender of our life and our will should be fulfilled, and then that the essential house-cleaning job should be completed, so that we are freed from our imprisonment and can "gild the more stately mansions, O my soul, as the swift seasons roll."

To build thus requires that we cease not only our bottle worship, but also that of the false Gods of money, power, sex, and self. All the chaos of today is manmade, in contrast to the universe about us which is so coordinated and orderly that all natural phenomena, when sufficiently studied and sufficiently understood, can be expressed by mathematical formulae.

It naturally follows that when we finally surrender our bloated ego to that Power greater than ourselves, and live out the will of the Creator Artist of the universe, that both the chaos and the inner conflict move out of our lives as harmony and beauty take their place.

Let us strive to keep before us the basic necessity and humility of our total surrender to our God, both in our daily program and when we carry through our sacred trust of sponsorship; in order that the afflicted coming after us will have a stately mansion for their refuge. As our Book says: "This is the how and why of it. First of all, we had to quit playing God. It didn't work. Next, we decided that hereafter in this drama of life, God was going to be our Director. He is the Principal; we are His agents. He is the Father, and we are His children. Most good ideas are simple, and this concept was the keystone of the new and triumphant arch through which we passed to freedom."[32]

THE JOURNEY INWARD TO FIND SPIRITUALITY
Humility Opened The Door

A new sponsoree sat at the foot of my bed. "Make me spiritual," she said. "I want to have what you have."

How do we become spiritual? For me, it has been a long, slow, continuous process. Some days, there were only one pair of footprints in the sand—it is an evolvement.

In the Big Book, we are told that to remain sober and be happy we must clean house, love God, and serve others. Cleaning house is the first step to finding the God within ourselves.

We do this by practicing Step Four—*Made a searching and fearless moral inventory of ourselves*. We search our past to see where we have spiritually, emotionally, physically, or financially harmed others. From this process, we develop **integrity**.

Many of us reached a state of moral decay and honesty was very difficult. We wondered if we could be "totally incapable of being honest." We shared this inventory with another person and we developed **courage**.

How good it feels!! Then we began to see our shortcomings as we swallowed our pride and started the ongoing process of working the Sixth and Seventh Step. At last, we began to have some **humility**. And, wonder upon wonder, humility opened the door to the Grace of God!! "The Journey Inward" had begun.[33]

MY NEED FOR GOD
Trusting God's Presence

I understand that the reason we find words like "Higher Power," "God as I understand Him," and "a Power greater than myself" in AA literature is so we each have a choice of finding our own spiritual comfort zone, at our own pace. I have read that in the very early days of AA the **God Power** of the program was strongly stressed when working with new alcoholics.

It wasn't until it became obvious that to bring a God that they had abandoned so long ago back into the picture too early, sent many of them scurrying out the door.

Quite frequently at meetings I hear members express problems with the Third Step. Usually that they try to turn things over to God, but soon find they have taken them back. As sharing continues, you hear a lot about growing up, being taught that God was a punishing God. Others tell of coming from a home where God was barely mentioned, and scarcely believed in. Or, as in my case where I had made so many promises that I had never kept, I didn't feel He wanted to ever hear from me again. In all cases, however, God had been put way into the background during a lot of drinking years.

They claim with the disease of alcoholism, first we lose our spiritual values, then our emotional stability, and the last to go is our health. In recovery, however, the process is reversed. First our health improves, then our emotional soundness, and the last to be restored is our spiritual health. With me it was a long time before I could truly feel a closeness, a true feeling of friendship, and a total trust that God was at my side. If I was consistent with my meditations, giving God time to talk to me, the answers to my problems seemed to find their way into my mind.

I think the first time I began to believe that God was really working in my life was when I came to realize that many of the things I had asked God to change in me had been changed. I had no recollection of doing anything myself other than praying to God that changes be made. To be honest, there was little credit I could claim for myself, even in the fact I had stopped drinking.

I like to compare my need for God in my life to walking out on a dock when the waves are passing underneath. The dock can be ever so sturdy and ever so wide, but all of a sudden I feel like my equilibrium is going to fail me. I can reach out and put my hand on another person, and the feeling will leave. I can walk out to the edge of a cliff and peer down at the depths below and the same feeling will overcome me. I can reach out and take hold of the smallest twig and then feel secure. I have to know there is some strength and touch my God physically. I can't turn and see Him visibly, but I can touch Him and see Him spiritually. I can't intellectualize my trust in my God. I only know He is there because my insides tell me He is there. I know that by **whatever name I call God, He will always be the same.**[7]

SPIRITUAL RATHER THAN RELIGIOUS
A Simple Way Of Living

People who are recovering from alcoholism or other addictions through Twelve Step programs hear phrases such as "the spiritual part of the program" or "this is a spiritual program." Twelve Step programs clearly separate themselves from religions and, yet, are equally clear in claiming to be spiritual programs. What does it mean to be "spiritual rather than religious"?

One simple way of understanding spirituality is to see that it is concerned with our ability, through our attitudes and actions, to relate to others, to ourselves, and to God as we understand Him. All of us, addicted or not, have a way of relating to our own lives, other people, and God which tends either to be positive, healthy, fulfilling and life-giving, or tends toward the negative, self-defeating, and destructive. The question is not whether we will be spiritual, but whether we are moving in the direction of a negative or positive spirituality.

Spirituality is a simple way of living. It seems there are four basic movements that recovering people need to make to put their lives on a positive spiritual basis. The first of these is a movement from fear to trust; the second, from self-pity to gratitude; the third, from resentment to acceptance; and the fourth, from dishonesty to honesty.[12]

III. PRAYER AND MEDITATION

THE MYSTERIES OF MEDITATION
How Does One Meditate?

"Sought through prayer and meditation to improve our conscious contact with God as we understood Him, . . ."

Most of us will instantly recognize the above as an extract from the Eleventh Step. The problem is its application. We all know how to pray. The point is, just how does one meditate?

Think about it for a while.

Yes, indeed, the proverbial million dollar question, undoubtedly asked by hundreds of thousands of floundering souls over the ages. The stumbling block to spiritual growth and serenity. Is this fact or supposition? Bill Wilson (co-founder of our fellowship and the main author of the Big Book, *Alcoholics Anonymous*) wrote as follows, in an article published in the June 1958 issue of the *Grapevine*:

> Sometimes, when friends tell us how well we are doing, we know better inside. We know we aren't doing well enough. We still can't handle life, as life is. There must be a serious flaw somewhere in our spiritual practice and development. What, then, is it? The chances are better than ever that we shall locate our trouble in our misunderstanding or neglect of AA's Step Eleven—prayer, meditation, and the guidance of God. The other steps can keep most of us sober and somehow functioning. But Step Eleven can keep us growing, if we try hard and work at it continually.

Having stressed the importance of meditation we look to our authoritative source, our textbook to living, the Big Book, *Alcoholics Anonymous*, for instructions on how to meditate.

In discussion of the Eleventh Step (from base of page 85 to the end of page 88) our Big Book mentions, "It would be easy to be vague about this matter. Yet, we believe we can make some definite and valuable suggestions." It then suggests (in essence): We do some self-searching, use our imaginations positively, resist morbid reflection, pray for strength and inspiration, relax, and listen for an intuitive thought or decision.

About fifteen years after the appearance of the Big Book, Bill Wilson wrote the *Twelve and Twelve*. AAs are often heard to say that the two works are contradictory, but the factual position is that the *Twelve and Twelve* embodies that many years more experience in sobriety. If anything, the *Twelve and Twelve* should be seen as an extension to or broadening of the basic principles and philosophies spelled out in the Big Book.

On meditation, in the *Twelve and Twelve*, Bill kicks off likewise:

> The actual experience of meditation and prayer across the centuries is, of course, immense. The world's libraries and places of worship are a treasure trove for all seekers. It is hoped that every AA who has a religious connection which emphasizes meditation will return to the practice of that devotion as never before. But what about the rest of us who, less fortunate, don't know how to begin?

He then proceeds to suggest a course of action to be followed to meditate. He says we should look for a good written prayer; that we reread the prayer several times, slowly savouring every word and trying to take in the deep meaning of each phrase and idea, then relax and breathe deeply the spiritual atmosphere with which the prayer surrounds us; let us become willing to partake and be strengthened and uplifted by the sheer spiritual power and love of which the prayer's magnificent words are carriers.

Beautiful, simply beautiful, but, alas, here is the rub. Alcoholism is also a spiritual disease and many of us are too battle-scarred to indulge in such sentimental drivel. Where does that leave us—are we debarred from meditation? Not necessarily, for the *Twelve and Twelve* again refers to the various components of meditation (those mentioned in the Big Book). Perhaps our lives can be radically changed for the better by spending a while each day in self-searching, seeking of higher values or the positive use of our imaginations, resisting morbid reflection, prayer, relaxation, and keeping our minds open to intuitive thoughts or ideas.

Remember, nobody holds the monopoly on meditation. It is something that can be individually developed, and one of its first fruits is emotional and spiritual balance.

ANOTHER KIND OF FLIGHT
Angels Can Fly Because
They Take Themselves Lightly

Alone and addicted, we were grounded, heavy, mired in our cravings. Feet embedded in quicksand, we engaged in mental flight—often fleeing from ourselves, from relationships, from bills and responsibility. Fleeing from one job to another, one spouse to another, one home to another, trying to escape our fears.

Once we believe, or are even **willing** to believe, in a power greater than ourselves, we can begin another kind of flight. We can leave behind the ballast that kept us down, stuck in the mud. We are free to soar and float and ride roller coasters in the sky. From there our vision is clearer, our perspective changed. Empowered by others and our belief in God as we understand God, we can transcend our personal limitations.

If we practice the Twelve Steps and do nothing more than that, we will be led gently into an increasingly rich relationship with a Higher Power of our choosing. All the ideas shared in this pamphlet are contained within the Twelve Steps of AA, as I understand them. My own relationship with a Higher Power develops as I practice these Steps.

Together, the Steps lead us into our rhythm of recovery—action and letting go, groundwork, and simply "being." They clearly define our part in a relationship with a Higher Power—what we do and what we ask our Higher Power to do. They help us define the nature of our relationship—one based on work and love. There is a Power greater than our limited, ego-based selves. We are free at any time to open up the lines of communication and become conscious of our natural, truly liberating connection.[13]

THE POWER OF PRAYER
Spiritual Medication For The Sick Soul

There are two types of diseases that are in absolute contrast to each other. In one type the cause of the disease is the presence of germs or bacteria that are harmful to the human body. The other type of disease is caused by the absence of some chemical or some other vital substance that is essential to keep the body from becoming disordered. Many human ills are deficiency diseases and can only be overcome by supplying those elements which are lacking.

So, in the first disease the germs must be destroyed or expelled before the body can be restored to good health. And in the second case, the body can only be brought back to good health by supplying the vital elements which it lacks. The alcoholic is a sick person. He is suffering from a physical and spiritual disease, but if he is fortunate enough to be hospitalized or if he can afford to pay a doctor, he will get medication for his illness. His doctor will give him medication to kill the germs that are harmful. And if he is suffering from the lack of the health giving elements, he will be given vitamin shots to replenish the deficiency of the vital elements that his body needs.

But his doctor cannot give him medication to bring his sick soul back to spiritual and moral health. He will have to seek spiritual medication from the Divine doctor. He is just as sick in his soul as he is in his body and he needs Divine medication to destroy the germs that are causing his mental turmoil. And he needs spiritual vitamins to restore his moral and spiritual deficiencies and build up his resistance to ward off the harmful germs.

Prayer is the vitamin for the sick soul. Prayer will kill the germs that are detrimental to man's soul. Prayer will restore humility and expel the germ of selfishness. It will destroy the germ of hate and restore the element of love. It will banish the germ of doubt and suspicion and restore faith. Daily prayer for the soul is like a daily vitamin for the body. It will restore our moral and spiritual deficiencies.

The health of our soul is just as important as the health of our body. The two go together. Physical power and vast possessions will not give us spiritual satisfaction unless we learn to use them to enrich our spiritual welfare. We may live in a mansion surrounded by every conceivable luxury and yet be poor in our family relationship for lack of love and sympathy. We may accumulate vast sums that will satisfy every whim, and yet be poor in real satisfaction unless we include the vitamin of prayer in our daily diet.

We are living in a civilization that has all the material wealth to make man happy and comfortable, yet with all this wealth there is spiritual poverty. We need something more than material things and body comfort to build up our spiritual health against the forces of evil. We need the vitamin of prayer in a world where so many demands are made upon us by the hucksters of depravity. Our scientific and modern civilization with all its marvels is suffering for lack of faith in God, without which our physical and material progress is in vain. "Yes, we have life, but we need something that will give meaning to Life."[16]

HOW TO GET THE RIGHT ANSWERS
Silent Prayer And Meditation

Sometimes newcomers to our Fellowship seem to be wrapped up in knots. They have problems they consider insoluble, unsolvable, and dismal.

How do you solve your problems? How do you reach answers for yourself?

Some seem to find solace in "the moment of silence followed by The Serenity Prayer" which opens most meetings.

How much silent meditation do you have every day? In the crisp, sharp air of silence you can hear your heart beat. When you read The Big Book, do you do it in silence or is your reading accompanied by the work-a-day sounds of the world all around?

Have you ever attended a Quaker meeting?

As the Quakers often practice, a group sits in complete silence for a lengthy period of time. The Quakers seek "peace at the center."

It is their belief that only out of peace at the center can you develop driving energy and consummate force. So sitting in silence they condition their minds.

Silent prayers and silent mediation are found in all major religions around the world. Why?

Dr. Norman Vincent Peale calls lengthy periods of silence, "listening to what God has to say in a serene way."

Robert Louis Stevenson wrote he could "drop the germ of an idea into the subconscious to germinate." When his brain cells had finished the idea would bubble back up completed. In this way, he said, he worked out some of his most unforgettable stories.

Albert Einstein admitted he applied himself to hard thinking then forgot his problem with his conscious mind, allowing the subconscious to work on it. Later, while doing something unrelated, a solution would suddenly surface.

When you have a problem, think it through. Then "Let Go and Let God."

Many great people are convinced God converses often with your subconscious mind, in silence.

MEDITATION
The Flowering Of The Action Taken

As with most everything in my recovery, I had no under-standing or correct experience of meditation when I came to AA. My mind was a roaring maelstrom; I could not keep still. Yet, applying Steps One through Ten settled and cleansed me enough to begin to meditate, and meditation has become, for me, the most sweet flowering of the action taken in those first Ten Steps.

The Eleventh Step information in the *12x12* has been extremely instructive to me. It provides an excellent beginning for meditation. The notion that meditation specifically expands God-consciousness appeals to me and summarizes my own meditative experience. The *12x12* also encourages me to seek "instruction and example" in meditation, and I have done so with results which only God could have planned.

Interestingly it was the first part of Step Eleven which really impelled me toward meditation. As I recognized the absolute need for prayer in recovery, I began to sit quietly in the morning and evening to speak with God. Then I noticed that after praying, I would remain poised in an inner spaciousness, calm and serene—meditating. However, my noisy alcoholic mind very often disturbs that meditative space. Jobs, relation-ship, family, and a thousand other living concerns will invade the quiet with demands for immediate attention. The many and varied meditation techniques prescribe effective methods for dealing with an unruly mind, but I have learned that whatever intrudes upon my meditation must be scrutinized with the help of the other Steps. What seeks precedence over my relationship with God, if not my cunning illness? Character defects constantly confront me in meditation. I try to take note and let them be until I can take suitable action.

There is no practice dearer to me than meditation. Through a persistent working of Step Eleven, I have begun to experience in my own heart the feeling of love and the promise of peace which I had always thought that alcohol would provide. As our Big Book states so simply and wisely on page 55:

> Sometimes we had to search fearlessly, but He was there. He was as much a fact as we were. We found the Great Reality deep down within us. In the last analysis it is only there that He may be found. It was so with us.[28]

AN ELEVENTH STEP STORY
Making The Effort

As with Step Ten, this step has been an off-again, on-again process for me. The most consistent thing I have done in my sobriety, besides go to meetings, is pray.

Before the beginning, I prayed, unknowingly, the principle of the Eleventh Step. Two years before I got sober, I began to pray for God's will for me and continued to drink. My drinking was horrendous those last two years. Finally after a year and a half, I had a glimmer of honesty—I realized that I was terrified of the will of God. As a cradle-Catholic, I knew what happened to those who experienced God's will—they were crucified, celibate, or both. I wished to be neither. So I added to my prayer for the will of God in my life "give me the grace to bear it." I knew it would be awful! (That old idea has been removed—mostly.) Within six months, I had my last drink. It worked! When I got here, I used the Serenity Prayer like a mantra about 35,000 times a day, because that's how often I was in pain! As I finally (almost 2 years later) began to work the program as set forth in our Basic Text, I began to read pages 83-88 in the Big Book each morning. It was about this same time that it was given to me—not in pain, this time, but in glorious gratitude to my God—to pray on my knees and out loud. I began to do that each morning and night, using the Third and Seventh Step prayers. I continue that practice up to this very day. Today I have a partner who is walking this path and we begin each morning we can with prayer together. I am grateful to be able to share this vital part of my life with another of God's special kids.

When I told my sponsor back then that I was (1) terrified and (2) on my knees at least once every day, he let me know that if I were taking the latter action, I needn't be afraid, because I was being taken care of.

Meditation has been a much sketchier deal for me. At first I thought that meditation was 15 minutes of "total" Nirvana. My alcoholic mind wouldn't shut up for a heartbeat. So . . . being a real one—"if I can't do it perfectly right off the bat, I won't do it!" My God is so creative. One day I made the effort. I had just sat and gotten quiet for a few minutes when the phone rang. As I stomped off to answer it, cursing all the way, a quiet voice inside said, "That's all you have to do—you just have to make the effort." For me, meditating in the evening, just before I go to bed, works best. I have also found help in some of those "many helpful books" and religious people that Bill W. mentions in his suggestions. I have a daily meditation book which gives me a reading on which to focus. As my head starts to drag me down the path, I bring my attention back to the passage at hand. I have not done this consistently and long enough to get to "total" anything. But as I practice, I do experience peace, security and a deep inner knowing that my God is HERE in my life, doing for me what I can't do for myself. I feel as refreshed as if I had just taken a two-week vacation. It's terribly practical—as is the rest of the program. I'm more OK with the fact that I'm not perfect at it—progress is the point—what else have I got to do with the rest of my life, but practice? And I have a Great Teacher who teaches me as I do—willingness is **action**—and "practice makes progress" as a neat Al-Anon told me.[28]

IV. THE SERENITY PRAYER

THE THINGS I CAN'T CONTROL

The true measurement of a person is not found in the ability to articulate a problem. The true measurement of a person is found in the ability to accept that which is beyond one's control and to change that which is within one's control.

Almost anyone can describe a problem. But to just dwell upon the problem without taking some course of action is to drain not only oneself but also those who happen to be unfortunate victims who experience the ventilation. We have all experienced at some time or another Mr. or Mrs. Griper, who is forever complaining about something. You see them coming and you go the other way. Such people keep digging themselves into a hole, and when they reach bottom, they continue to dig.

There are certain things we have no control over, such as the weather. So if it rains, there is no need to stand around complaining. Rather, we accept the fact the picnic needs to be cancelled and we move on to an alternate plan.

Spiritually mature people who experience that which is beyond their control see the situation not as a problem but as a challenging opportunity from which they can learn and grow. The man who travelled across the country in a wheelchair serves as a source of inspiration and forces us to be introspective, asking ourselves, "Do I have the spiritual fortitude he had?"

Often life's challenging opportunities seem so overwhelming to us we throw our hands up in a gesture of powerlessness. Such issues as world hunger and peace sometimes seem so far beyond our individual control we are tempted to throw in the towel. In such times I must remind myself—God is calling me to be faithful, not to save the world. All I am expected to do is my best in facing these challenging opportunities of life no matter how insignificant my effort may appear to be. As I think about it, there are many things within my immediate grasp to control—my attitude, dieting, exercise, and how I will act and react to others' behavior.

Life showers challenging opportunities upon all of us. Some things we have no control over, so we accept them, learn and grow from them, and still do our best in spite of the odds. Things we can control, particularly ourselves, we commit ourselves to controlling. May God give us the wisdom to know the difference.

THE SERENITY PRAYER
Ask Only For Wisdom

How many of us say this little prayer at the start of an AA meeting and promptly forget it ? This is the most powerful short prayer in the world today. Nothing can replace the Lord's Prayer, of course, but these words of the Serenity Prayer pack a lot of power and meaning.

GOD	With the saying of this word, we are admitting the existence of a Higher Power.
GRANT	With the repeating of this second word we are admitting that this Higher Power is an authority that can **bestow** or **give**.
ME	We are asking something for ourselves, for the Bible states "Ask and it shall be given." It is not wrong to ask for betterment of yourself, for with the improvement of your character people around you will be made happier.
SERENITY	We are asking for **calmness, composure,** and **peace** in our lives which will enable us to think straight and govern ourselves properly.
TO ACCEPT	We are resigning ourselves to conditions as they are right now.
THINGS I CANNOT CHANGE	We are accepting our lot in life as it is. Until we have the courage to change part of our lives we don't like, we must accept it and **not accept it grudgingly** .

COURAGE   We are asking for a quality of spirit to face conditions without flinching.

TO CHANGE   We are asking for conditions to be different.

THE THINGS I CAN   We are asking for help to make a right decision. If you have to make a decision, consider carefully the worst that could happen to you **if your decision to change did not work out.** If you can accept the worst and your decision can get you out of a rut, then proceed.

WISDOM   We are asking for the ability to form sound judgments in any matter.

TO KNOW   We want to understand clearly a truth of fact.

THE DIFFERENCE   We want to see things differently in our lives so there can be some distinction. We need to sense a definite value in sobriety over drunkenness if we are to stay sober.

Help me, O Lord, when I want to do the right thing but know not what it is. But help me most, dear Lord, when I know perfectly well what I ought to do, but can't find "the will to do it."

Ask only in life for wisdom.
All other things follow in line.

WHAT IS SERENITY?

SERENITY—is not freedom from the storms of life. It is the calm in the middle of the storm that gets me through.

SERENITY—is not something that protects me from hard times. It is a special kind of strength that helps me to face my problems and work through them.

SERENITY—is at hand when I learn to **Let Go and Let God**. Then I will have time to count my blessings, work on my shortcomings, and enjoy one day at a time.

SERENITY—helps me **accept** the fact that I can't change another human being.

SERENITY—gives me **courage** to change the things I can. I can't change anyone else, but I can change myself and my attitudes.

HOW TO ACHIEVE SERENITY!

I will separate, in my mind, the sickness of alcoholism from the person who suffers from it.

I must transform good resolutions into good habits.

I will not let my inner peace be disturbed by confusion around me.

I will be gentle and tolerant, while maintaining my right to individuality.

I will listen and appreciate, and not judge the source of what I hear.

I will stop reacting to everything that occurs. When I react, I put the control of my peace of mind in the hands of others.

SERENITY = UNITY WITH GOD'S WILL

I am continually surprised at the number of AA members who are resentful because they have not acquired "serenity." They can't get peace of mind "no matter how they try."

It is my opinion and it has certainly been my experience that we don't "get" serenity by fighting for it or even by looking for it. In fact, we may even lose it by wanting it!

Why? Again, in my opinion, serenity or peace of mind is not a goal in itself. It is the result of a revolution in our thinking; a revolution, in our case, brought about by our efforts to apply the Twelve Steps of the AA program to our daily life.

I heard a real old-timer the other night say that the Twelve Steps are really one step, divided into twelve pieces. Of course the First Step is essential to sobriety and without it the whole program collapses. But the core of the program is the Third Step. And the heart of the difficulty we have in applying it is our increasing desire to run the show in our own way.

We lose our serenity in the hardship and anguish we suffer every day from the burden of our own selfishness and clumsiness and incompetence and pride. Discouraged by our own failures, we are hungry to be led and advised and directed by someone else. Who? The Third Step answers the question. *"Made a decision to turn our will and lives over to the care of God as we understood Him."*

Our own will has become the source of so much misery and darkness, that we renounce our own will, our own ego and pride and desire and seek God's will for us. When we do this we find peace and serenity even in the midst of labor and conflict and trial.

Serenity is impossible for the man who is dominated by all the confused and changing desires of his own will. And even if those desires reach out for the good things of life, for peace and recollection, or the pleasures of prayer, if they are no more than natural desires, they will make serenity difficult or even impossible.

It is unlikely then that we will have perfect serenity or peace of mind unless we are detached from even the desire for serenity. We may never be able to pray perfectly unless we detach ourselves from the desire for the pleasures of prayer.

The secret of serenity then is detachment from our own will. That is worth repeating: The secret of serenity is detachment from our own will. If we attach importance to our own desires, we run the risk of losing what is essential to serenity—the acceptance of God's will, no matter what our feelings happen to be.

Detachment. If we think that the most important thing in life is serenity, we become all the more disturbed when we notice we do not have it. And because we cannot directly produce serenity in ourselves when we want it, our disturbance increases with the failure of our efforts. Finally, losing patience by refusing to accept this situation which we cannot control, we climb into the driver's seat and lose the one important reality—union with God's will without which serenity is nearly impossible.

It is important then to revolutionize our thinking about the importance of the human will—our own human will in particular. I heard it expressed once as the laying down of our will alongside God's will so that the two become as one.

Just how we accomplish this is what makes the individual aspect of the AA program. For each of us comes into AA with a different temperament, a different background, and various reactions to our past experiences.

One thing I think is important in setting goals for yourself: do not become too disturbed at failure. We are all far from perfect. If we expect to achieve perfection we shall certainly be disappointed. Peace of mind and serenity do come to us in proportion as we turn our lives and wills over to the care of God, as we understand him, but don't look for it and crave it. If you think serenity is a great and wonderful thing and that it makes you superior to other men, then you cannot desire it as it ought to be desired. It is necessary to be abased, not to be exalted. It is not helpful to be great in your own eyes but to be little.

For it is in humility that you find the answer to all the great problems of life and the soul.[34]

OUR AA PRAYER

"God grant me the serenity to *accept* the things I cannot change, courage to *change* the things I can, and wisdom to *know* the difference."

Have you considered how much can be gained by reading this supplication with your heart as well as with your eyes and mind? Let's take a closer look at this prayer, one so important, in fact, all important to alcoholics.

"God grant me the serenity to accept the things I cannot change." We must ask God for serenity, because only in God can we find it. We may seek it through humans, but they create confusion and turmoil, whereas God is serenity. Hence, we ask God for serenity to accept the things we cannot change, such as weather, death, illness, sorrow—the things of life that are beyond our power. We must accept them with serenity, for if we don't, we have the frustrating sensation of butting our heads against brick walls.

We cannot make the sun shine if it is cloudy, but we can have sunshine radiating from our faces if it is in our hearts; we cannot bring back the dead, but we can live our own lives in such a way as to spend eternity in their company. We cannot heal incurable disease, but we can pray that the afflicted persons may gain the serenity to accept his plight and be delivered from pain. If we have God-given serenity we have no need for drink.

"Courage to change the things I can." If we should see a suffering soul and do nothing to alleviate that suffering, we are totally without courage. Who can pass an injured person without helping, or a crippled pencil-vendor without dropping

a coin into his little tin cup? Who can live with himself or herself, if he or she knows they are wrong, admits it, and yet perversely, does nothing about it? It takes little courage to call an ambulance or drop a coin into a tin cup, but it takes lots of courage to change one's self into the person one has potential to be. That, indeed, takes courage, and where are we to gain this courage if not from God? It takes courage to attend a party and refuse that first drink, knowing someone may laugh; but you also know you dare not take it or all is lost.

"And wisdom to know the difference." There are many things you can change, you think, but it takes wisdom to know whether or not you can. For instance, can you change another's way of thinking? You can, by example, if by no other method. But sometimes a person does not want to be changed. If you recognize this you have gained the wisdom to differentiate. The things you cannot change. They are the items mentioned above; the things only God, in His Infinite Power, controls. As long as we cannot change them, why not channel our efforts into something worthwhile, that is helping our fellow-man. It all reverts to serenity, that magic state of mind—that inner peace we gain only from God. So God enters non-religious AA; He enters because we in AA realize that we need Him, perhaps more than ordinary unafflicted human beings. In our meetings we use this little serenity prayer. Between times when you feel your serenity slipping, take time to repeat it silently to yourself and to Him.

Happiness is a habit, a by-product of right thinking and living. Live a simple life. Spend less than you earn. Think constructively. Cultivate a yielding disposition and resist the common tendency to want things your own way. Be grateful. Rule your moods, cultivate a mental attitude of peace and good will. Give generously; there is no greater joy in life than to render happiness to others by means of intelligent giving. Work with right motives. Be interested in others and divert your mind from self-centeredness. Live one day at a time by making the most of today. Keep close to God, as you understand God. True and enduring happiness depends primarily upon close alliance with Him.

v. PERSONAL SHARING

RATIONALIZERS
We Must Straighten Out Our Thinking

Alcoholics are as erratic as the English language. The trouble with alcoholics is that they are not rational. Now rational means to be sensible and reasonable. It denotes the ability to think and reason clearly.

That's why the Big Book says we must straighten out our thinking. Irrational thinking is the basis of our trouble. But here is where the quirk comes in—both in the alcoholic and the language.

Too often alcoholics begin to rationalize. While this word comes from the word rational it has been twisted by usage to mean the making of excuses, the formulation of alibis, and downright lying.

It is awfully easy for the alcoholic to go beyond being rational and start to rationalize. All of us have encountered some outstanding examples.

There are the persons who use Alcoholics Anonymous as a sobering up station. They have sunk pretty far down the slide. They are in trouble at home and at work, possibly even with the law. They cry out for help and get it.

What happens in such cases? They come out of the fog and they want to take charge of the world again. The tears and hand wringing of five or six days before are forgotten. The "Thank the Almighty for such friends as you" go by the boards. The promise to abide by the rules and take it gradually is not recalled. They even get angry if you remind them of it. They're feeling swell again. Why should they put themselves under any obligation—especially the insulting one of taking an inventory and trying to remedy any defects of character. Me? Defects of character? Are you nuts?

This is what is known as stinking thinking. This is rationalization of the first water.

There's the person, too, who takes a superficial attitude toward AA. He attends because his family or his employer more or less compels him to. He flits around the perimeter of the group. Pleasant enough as an individual, he never does a lick of work in any form. And as far as putting himself out, taking time and energy, to help sober up another alcoholic—never.

In fact, he can't. He hasn't got the program himself to begin with. He is in the same class as the rationalizer who is always making excuses, either verbally for everyone to hear, or mentally through his own limited cranial processes.

These examples, which are almost standard, and others which any of us could cite, should underscore a basic truth: Alcoholics Anonymous is not a way-station for troubled drunks. It is a program for a new way of life that can function only in the individual, by the individual, and for the individual.

There are plenty of cures and rest homes and agencies that can handle the persons who want to call an intermission in their drinking, but Alcoholics Anonymous is not one of them. Alcoholics Anonymous was devised for the men and women who, through bitter experience, have determined to change their lives, alter their characters and give of themselves to help others.

This society came into being to help those of us who sincerely wish to become rational, to do something on our own initiative and with the help of a Higher Power and our fellow travelers, to make our lives orderly and decent. It is not a haven for the alibi artist, the excuse expert or the irrational rationalizer.[4]

RESENTMENT = POISON

Resentment is a deadly poison that seems to plague us all at times, even after some time of sobriety, a problem that will no doubt plague us most of our lives. AA does try to help us become aware of its dangers.

AA has taught me that:
1. Resentment robs me of serenity.
2. Resentment makes happiness impossible.
3. Resentment uses up energy that could go into accomplishment.
4. Resentment can become an emotional habit, making us habitually feel that we are victims of injustice.
5. Resentment is an emotional rehashing of some event or circumstance of the past. You cannot win because you cannot change the past.
6. Resentment is not caused by other persons, circumstances or events, but by our own emotional response.

One way to handle resentment is to decide how much resentment the person, circumstance, or event deserves (which is usually very little) or how much I need to suffer. With resentment, like anger, nobody suffers but me.

Then I have to say to myself, "Who needs it!", and call someone in AA and go to a meeting.[7]

THOSE OLD TIRED SLOGANS

A wag once said, "There's nothing wrong with this world that a good cliche won't cure!" When I was early on in the program, I had progressed to the point where I was feeling good. Things were getting better. But this was before I had accepted the program fully and unconditionally, not questioning, analyzing, or criticizing.

But, every meeting I went to, someone—sometimes it seemed everyone—spoke with those old, tired slogans. I began to feel a little irritation, and intellectual arrogance, at this lack of originality. I just knew that the use of these was for minds that were running on empty and needed someone else's pre-digested philosophy. Oh sure, the program seemed to work OK, but maybe it needed a little fine-tuning. **If It Works, Don't Fix It!**

I like to analyze things—things material, spiritual, or mental. What makes it tick? Why does it work? **Utilize It, Don't Analyze It!** When I wondered about "How It Works," someone pointed out that it says **how** it works, not **why.** The founders of this program knew the men and women they were trying to save. The sick, suffering alcoholic does not need a philosophy debate. They need help. They need to be shown and told what they have to do, right now, to not take that next drink. **The Twelve Steps.**

And when they are over the whips and the jingles, they need to be shown the path that will keep them sober, clean up the past, and make each 24 hours a serene experience.

The first step mentions alcohol. The other eleven talk about living, living a life that is truly happy, joyous, and free.

After a year I went out. My misery was **cheerfully refunded**. Thank God, I got back to the Program.

Now, I understand things a lot better. My intellectual pride is still there. But it has room for the slogans. And I use them— because they work—and they make sense![35]

EMOTIONAL MATURITY

The mature person has developed attitudes in relation to themselves and their environment which has lifted them above "childishness" in thought and behavior.

Some of the characteristics of the person who has achieved true adulthood are suggested here:

1. They accept criticism gratefully, being honestly glad for an opportunity to improve.
2. They do not indulge in self-pity. They have begun to feel the laws of compensation operating in all life.
3. They do not expect special consideration from anyone.
4. They control their temper.
5. They meet emergencies with poise.
6. Their feelings are not easily hurt.
7. They accept the responsibility of their own acts without trying to "alibi."
8. They have outgrown the "all or nothing" stage. They recognize that no person or situation is wholly good or wholly bad, they begin to appreciate the Golden Mean.
9. They are not impatient at reasonable delays. They have learned that they are not the arbiter of the universe and that they must often adjust themselves to other people and their convenience.
10. They are good losers. They can endure defeat and disappointment without whining and complaining.
11. They do not worry unduly about things they cannot help.
12. They are not given to boasting or "showing off" in socially unacceptable ways.

13. They are honestly glad when others enjoy success or good fortune. They have outgrown envy and jealousy.
14. They are open-minded enough to listen thoughtfully to the opinions of others.
15. They are not chronic "fault-finders."
16. They plan things in advance rather than trusting to the inspiration of the moment.

Least of all, we think in terms of spiritual maturity.

1. They have faith in a Power greater than themselves.

2. They feel themselves an organic part of mankind as a whole, contributing their part to each group of which they are a member.

3. They obey the spiritual essence of the Golden Rule: "Thou shalt love their neighbor as thyself."

WHO BLOCKS YOU?
Character Defects

There is an old parable written many years ago by a sage in Central Europe which is timeless. It will have a point as long as man exists. It runs as follows:

Have you ever seen a horse drink at a brook? It strikes out with its front hoofs. Why this? It sees its own reflection and thinks that it is another horse that wants to drink up its water. But it is given to you to know: that in no other than yourself, you yourself stand in your way!

Had the author of that story been alive today we would say that either he was a member of Alcoholics Anonymous or very acquainted with the philosophy and the intent of the Twelve Steps.

The times are innumerable when, in drinking days, we acted like the horse. It was the other fellow who was to blame for what we did. We struck out at him. We fretted and worried because those sober ones would not leave us alone. They were always after us and we were embittered and we justified what we did because of them.

Not until we attained sobriety did we realize that these "others" were wholly imaginary, that they were reflections of our own thinking, our own defects of character, and we were using them as excuses and alibis to justify our moods and actions.

Looking back it all seems rather silly that we should have no more wit than a horse gazing at its own image in a brook. As we laugh at it we also give thanks that we have escaped from the thralldom of such illusions, that we have attained the good sense to recognize the source of our trouble in ourselves. But in being amused we should keep in mind an ever present danger—that such moods can and do recur and often put us in a state of mind where we revert to the feeling that, since things are not going just as we would wish, or someone has hurt our pride or dented our ego, other people are to blame.

Some few members of AA may escape these black moods and these dry binges, but most of us are subject to them through the years. We must take them into account and be prepared to meet them. They can come at the most unexpected times and for the most trivial of reasons. They can—and unfortunately on occasion have—thrown a person back on the vicious, hopeless resource of alcohol.

In our experience these periods occur when we are over-tired, when pressures and tensions have mounted and conse-quently our guard is down. They come when relations with family, business associates, and friends were negative or ad-verse. Then some remark or some action of no real importance can trigger the mood.

Once again we act like the poor horse and kick the water and make things unpleasant and messy all around us. When it's over we are a bit ashamed of our thoughts and attitudes and actions. How do we guard against it? One imperative way is in working on character defects continuously. None of us is so perfect that there isn't abundant room for improvement. In calm moments of reflection we are highly conscious of this. Another way is to remember that whatever mood we get in it will not last. We must learn to view these periods as temporary aberrations in our thinking. In doing so we can meet them head on and not suffer them out in grouchy tantrums. In doing this the moods become of shorter duration and their recurrence less frequent.

None of us, however, can sit back and not work at this problem under the illusion that it never will arise again. We are still alcoholics with the tendencies, even when sober, that the name implies. There is no sense in continuing to be the block to our own efforts at recovery.[4]

THE 12 STEPS HELP US
ELIMINATE SHAME

A wise old woman in AA once told me that the emotion which forced the out-of-control drinking alcoholic most deeply into despair was not guilt but shame. And, she added, the greatest source known for conquering the feeling of shame is found in the principles and program of Alcoholics Anonymous.

Along the recovery road of reducing shame, the steps of AA and the sharing engaged in by those in its fellowship take care of the guilt that haunts us all the way to surrender and acceptance.

It should interest us in AA to know that guilt is mainly regretting what we have lost, while shame concerns what we have become. Guilt is the result of transgressions such as breaking rules of man and of God. Shame grows out of our shortcomings and failures.

With guilt, wrong-doers build a sense of wickedness. In shame, an inadequacy produces feelings of worthlessness. We believe we are no good. In most cases, we alcoholics feel both guilt and shame for the same error of commission or omission.

When drinking, guilt often forced us to reproach ourselves:

> "How could I have done such a thing to my friend?" With shame it was: "How could I have been so stupid and untrustworthy?" In other words, guilt is "What have I *done*?" while shame is "What have *I* done?"

In AA, we grow by experiencing shame through knowing that we have fallen short and by confessing that we have flaws of character rather than feeling we are sinful wrong-doers. AA thus can make shame a positive influence in our recovery. Our program assures us that "to be human is to be prone to having problems."

Since guilt results from voluntary acts and shame from the involuntary, AA puts the problem of a newcomer quickly into the shame division and immediately begins eliminating it. A beginner is told, "You are not immoral or wicked. You didn't always want to get drunk, but you did because you suffer from a disease. You are an alcoholic, and alcoholics are compelled to get drunk when they really don't want to."

It was natural for us drinkers to feel shame because we mistakenly relied on will-power to control our drinking. We automatically set ourselves up for failure because we tried to will something that can never be willed—moderation for the alcoholic.

When we drank, shame was our closely-guarded secret. We experienced it, but we fought to prevent its exposure. Among our reasons for drinking was to prove we needed no help from others. So we became dependent on alcohol. And, in hiding shame from others, we prevented the exposure of that shame even to ourselves. We ended up hiding not only shame but all of our other defects from ourselves.

AA promptly told us as newcomers to expose that shame to others—and hence to ourselves—by working the Steps. It became more important to share with others than to try to "cure" our disease. It became apparent that alcoholics are dependent on one another. We learned that others, too, had felt shame.

It was a revelation to discover that there is no shame in having felt ashamed, since it is true that "If we are to attain the heights of human existence, we must touch its depths."[9]

YOU'RE NOT REALLY BIG BOOK

Hi, Everybody! I'm an alcoholic and my name is Doug.
(Hi, Doug!)

I want to thank the committee for having me and that this
has been a marvelous, memorable, and really outstanding con-
ference. And those of you who wish to remember it that way
may want to leave now.

If you have a notion to leave, let me just give you the
message quickly. The book says I'm supposed to tell you what
I used to be like, not what "it" used to be like, what happened and
what I'm like now. To make a long story short, I used to be a
self-loathing drunk. What happened was I took the Steps the
best I could according to the method outlined in the Big Book
and today I'm self-respecting and sober. And that's it! And now
I'm going to stay a while and talk.

Has anyone else in the audience had trouble with a sponsee
not understanding what you say? They have a tendency to go out
and do exactly the opposite of whatever I've suggested to do
next and come back and say "It worked." I have sponsorship
down now to page numbers. A pigeon will call me and I'll tell
them to go home and read page 98 in the Big Book. Sometimes
my wife will say, "Doug, what's on page 98?" And I'll answer,
"I don't know—words." Next day my pigeon will call again and
tell me that's exactly what he needed and then I have to put him
on hold and go read page 98.

The speakers before me today and yesterday have all
mentioned and quoted out of the Big Book. Which reminds me
of a fellow in Dallas who is no longer anonymous because he's
dead, but he died sober! Which will do wonders for you in AA.
This is the only fellowship on the face of the earth where you can

die divorced, under indictment, bankrupt, and disgraced; but if you die sober someone will come to your funeral and say, "There's a winner." And Dell was a winner.

I'm going to tell you a little story about Dell. Dell was so dogmatic, obnoxious, opinionated, offensive, hard headed, foul mouthed, and otherwise intransigent that he got whether he wanted it or not the nickname of "Big Book Dell." I became a camp follower of "Big Book Dell" and never had him as a sponsor but I got a lot of benefit from his sobriety. And I had another friend who had a reputation of being a Big Book "disciple" who took me aside one time and said, "Did you know that Dell isn't really Big Book?" And he told me his reasons why Dell wasn't really Big Book. So being a person who can keep a confidence and a lawyer to boot I went to Dell and asked him about the other guy who leads a Big Book study on the other side of town. And Dell said, "Well, he's not really Big Book." And then somebody told me why my sponsor wasn't really Big Book. And I asked my sponsor and he told me the guy who told me he wasn't really Big Book wasn't really Big Book.

I began a Big Book study group at my home group on Thursday nights and I'm studying along with the text and some people who Dell sponsors were there. I said something out of the Big Book and I can prove it in black and white and I heard one of Dell's sponsees say that I wasn't really Big Book and I then said that's it! "You ain't really Big Book until somebody says you ain't really Big Book." 'Cause what that really means is that the person who's not really Big Book has internalized the principles of the Big Book to the point that they can hold their own opinions and attitudes and speak their own truth without apology, hesitation, or equivocation and that alone makes you "Really Big Book."

When I went to my first AA meeting, a fellow came over and asked me how I was doing. I said that if I didn't get a drink in the next 15 minutes I'd die. He said, "Well let's go get a cup of coffee and see if you die!" Of course we did and I didn't. He asked me if there was something unmanageable going on in my head that made me think I was going to die? I came to the realization the unmanageability in my life had nothing to do with my credit rating, it was a matter of having the capability of being alone at perfect peace and ease. And if I don't there's something unmanageable going on in my head that makes me feel that way and that something is called alcoholism. Blaming alcohol for alcoholism is like blaming gas for car accidents. Alcohol is a substance that I treated my alcoholism with until it no longer worked. And when the solution itself became life threatening I came to AA When I stopped drinking I was the same person before I started drinking which was the reason I drank in the first place!

When you get to that place where you need to be restored to sanity it turns out that this is what AA promises. That there would be a Power greater than myself that could restore me to sanity. And I'm convinced that the recovery from alcoholism as taught by AA is a life long process. I've learned that I need to practice the principles of the Twelve Steps on a daily basis if I want to stay reasonably happy and generally useful while sober. I call this recovery and I believe it's possible with the program of AA to be content with sobriety and useful to others. This is outlined in the first 164 pages of the Big Book.

In closing I would like to remind myself that this program works because of a loving God working through people like you that I'm sober today and for that I thank you. Let's close with the Serenity Prayer.[15]

REAPING THE BENEFITS OF THE 12 STEPS

Since becoming a member of Alcoholics Anonymous, I have found that the Twelve Steps of this program of recovery have become a central part of my life. Although in my early days of recovery I could not remember one from the other, I have found that with time this changed and now these Twelve Steps have taken on a new meaning that I have condensed in the following way.

I believe the First Step has given me direction to be **honest with myself**. Until I adopted that principle, I could not accept the disease of alcoholism. But, when I did get honest with myself, AA and you people were placed in my life.

I don't believe we, as individuals, can do anything about our disease until we honestly know that we are sick.

The Second Step is **hope**, hope that there is a way to treat my disease and to remove the unmanageability in my life.

Step Three is **faith**. The definition of Faith, for me, is that although I don't know what is going to happen in my life, by trusting in God, I know it's going to be all right.

Step Four is **courage**, courage to change everything as it is explained in Chapter Two of the Big Book. I found that first I need to take an inventory of my character defects that need to be changed and then to use that awareness to trust my feelings and act on them.

Step Five is **integrity**, the state of being complete or whole. For me, this came by sharing the things that had kept my life in a shambles for so many years.

Step Six is **willingness** to have God remove all these defects. His Will not mine! As in the Serenity Prayer, it is also the willingness to change the things that need to be changed.

Step Seven is **humility**. Until I adopted humility in my life, my ego seemed to be out of control, and it was difficult to turn over my will and life to God. When I worked Step Seven and adopted Humility, I found that I was powerless over people, places, things, and situations. I realized the only thing left was that I could change my attitude toward them by turning my will over to that Power greater than myself.

Step Eight is **brotherly love**, a principle I had heard about, but was never able to understand until I worked Step Eight. Today I try to treat people as I want to be treated.

Step Nine is **discipline**, a very important principle to me as an alcoholic. Everything was out of control when I got here. Today, by disciplining myself to live one day at a time—live and let live, let go and let God, don't take the first drink, pray in the morning for guidance, pray in the evening thanking God for the day He has given me—my life continues to get better each day.

Step Ten is **perseverance**, my perseverance to make sure that by taking an inventory daily I can keep little things that bother me from becoming an anchor around my neck.

Step Eleven is the **awareness of the everpresence of God in my life today**. This is my pivotal step. Everything revolves around my conscious contact with God as I understand him. Spirituality.

Step Twelve is **service**. I've found that I have to keep it. There are many forms of service—sharing at meetings, being a *Grapevine* representative writing articles, sponsoring others, performing AA service work—but I believe the most important is showing up at meetings to be there for others when they reach out as AA was there for me. I am forever grateful that when I asked for help, you were there.

When I read the Twelve Steps or hear them read at meetings, I am reminded that I must continue to apply these principles in my life and to reach out my hand to the newcomer who walks into the meeting hall. Because we are all here to share the experience, strength, and hope of our sobriety.[14]

VISION FOR THE FUTURE: GRATITUDE

Probably my biggest sense of gratitude is for having been granted an increasing awareness of my self-destructive half, the acceptance of alcohol as a prime trigger for this and, finally, twelve channels to explore myself mentally, physically, spiritually, and emotionally in conjunction with everything else.

Defects of character—but for these this alcoholic doubts if he would have sustained his abuse of alcohol. AA teaches me to recognize my defects, the knowledge of which is so important in preventing me from repeating disasters from which I never learned. This is a gratitude born through self-examination and based on the observations of sober people. Further gratitude is felt for being sober now and for the fine vision for the future with its concepts of humility, Higher Power, simplicity, reality, and trust and many others.

I am learning to regard life as a loan which, like all loans, is to be returned. As a custodian it is incumbent upon me to tend it with care. Also, within the limits of my understanding and ability, I believe I must apply the right and seek the good, shun fear, and seek faith. With my fellow man I should seek love, dignity, and humility. At my end I hope to feel fulfillment and gratitude for the loan rather than malice, hate, fear, or failure.

I feel great beauty around me which I hope these thoughts convey. My effort has been well rewarded. I close with gratitude.[6]

WHERE DO I GO FROM HERE?
Overcoming Fear

Forty-three years ago I stood among my classmates with a new diploma in my hand. It was a happy occasion, but I had some strange feelings. They were very strong and very real, and I did not know what they were. Thirty-four years later I walked out of St. John's treatment center. I had not had a drink in five weeks. It was a happy occasion, but I had some strange feelings. I did not know what they were, but they were very strong and very real. In February of this year I walked out of the Fargo Clinic with some great news. Words just spoken by my doctor were still ringing in my ears, words that had to be called a miracle. It was a happy day, but I had feelings. I did not know what they were, but they were very strong and very real. As I walked to the car from the clinic door, I realized that what I was feeling was exactly the same as when I stood among my classmates, diploma in hand, wondering **where do I go from here?**

These thoughts stayed with me for days and I realized that I had felt the same way many times since I started dealing with feelings in treatment and in working my program over the years that followed. Naturally, a desire to identify these feelings came into my times of meditation, and as always the thoughts that seemed related to the problem started to stand out. So who was the bogey man? What basic feeling was I dealing with? I decided it was fear, fear that the good would not last, and the real task would be to once again overcome the bad that was sure to happen. This is when the real shocker came.

I always had thought of myself as a positive person. Did these new realizations label me a negative thinker? I guess I would have to admit that in a way it did. Once again I was 18 going on 62, dealing with something about myself that I had never faced before. During all those years of drinking the actions from which I claimed my strokes were by doing an acceptable job in spite of the hours of sleep missed after the poisoning of my system each night with volumes of liquor; then falling short of a task and manipulating myself away from the blame. With the help of booze I plowed my way through with an "I'll show them" attitude. All these accomplishments, however, were to overcome negative situations. None of them were taking the good news and making it greater. I have heard many times that alcoholics have a hard time accepting success. But I thought I did a great job accepting success: I got promoted, I got raises, I got recognition from the company, I exceeded sales goals. I accepted these successes proudly. It took me a while to realize that all these accomplishments were once again, overcoming negatives.

So what has my program taught me? I have learned that God wants me to be joyous, happy, and free, to dwell on the positive, and that it is OK to be good to me. The program has taught that I cannot have fear in the presence of Faith. Steps six, seven, and eleven can rid me of useless fear and strengthen my Faith. When I stood with my classmates with a new diploma, it was no time to fear failure. When I walked out of St. John's, it was not time to fear that the program would not work for me. When I walked out of the Fargo Clinic, it was no time to fear the cancer would return. Those were the times I should have taken the good news and made it better.

So where am I at today? I'm grateful I'm sober. I'm grateful I have a place to belong, friends who accept me, and a God that loves me and guides me. I can take all this good news and make it greater. That's **where I can go from here.**[7]

IF YOU SLIP—DON'T BLAME AA

If a diabetic fails to take his insulin and has another attack. If an ulcer patient does not follow his prescribed diet and has another attack. If a man with an arrested case of tuberculosis, fails to follow his doctor's advice with the result that the disease flares again.   If a person with heart trouble or high blood pressure ignores his physician's advice and has another attack.

We don't fire the doctor or say the medicine is no good. We send for the doctor and ask him to help us again.

If good church members sin, they don't fire the preacher, priest or rabbi, and say their religion's no good.

If you are an alcoholic and do "slip," don't be so foolish as to drop out of AA and say it is no good. Do as the patient does. Remember how well you got along while you followed the AA prescription. Then get back into AA and start getting along well again.

OUTLOOK OF TWO AA MEMBERS
A Question Of Attitudes

Don D. went to an AA meeting one evening. He frowned when a member mispronounced a few words while reading "How It Works." He felt appalled when another member stood up and said he was an alcoholic and an addict. Another person talked too long. As he slipped out the door immediately after the meeting, he muttered, "That was terrible. I should have stayed home."

Bob M. went to a meeting one evening. His head was bowed as he listened to the "Preamble" and "How It Works." His eyes moistened as he listened intently to a member tell his story. He was grateful for being able to attend this meeting. After clean-up and a little socializing, he paused, and as he locked the meeting room door, his thoughts were, "Thank God for such a beautiful fellowship."

Both AA members were at the same meeting. Each found what they were looking for.

WHO ARE THE WINNERS IN AA?

There's a lot they don't explain in AA. They keep telling you to "stick with the winners" and "make sure you become one of the winners." But they don't say exactly who or what a winner is, in AA terms. They just sort of leave you to work it out.

Well I've been wondering about it and what I'm wondering is this. Does not having a slip, keeping off the sauce for several years, and staying around the AA meetings make someone a winner? The reason I'm asking is because this means there are thousands and thousands of winners in AA, and as I take a look around it all gets pretty confusing. The reason it gets confusing is because there are so many different kinds of "winner" and I don't see how I can "stick with" and "become like" the whole lot of them. At least that's how it looks, and I'm not really sure if I've got this "winner" thing right.

For instance, a lot of members go on about the terrific changes in their lives since they've been sober. And the changes they go on about are their good jobs and all the compliments they get, and the big paychecks and nice houses and maybe even the new car and frequent vacations. And they talk about it all being due to AA and sobriety. They must be right, and it makes sobriety sound great so I suppose these AA members are considered to be very good "winners." But what I can't help wondering is this. How would they be making out with the program and sobriety if they lost their health and couldn't work or got landed with some other big thing that really put the gravy train into a siding? I mean, it's easy to smile when you've got plenty to smile about materially. So is it really the people who've got it all going for them who are the real winners?

Or are the winners the ones who are going like fury at the meetings? You know about five or more a week—here, there, and everywhere and getting home late? I know that every once in a while a lot of people need as many meetings as that, and I know too that it's the ones with years of sobriety who've got the most to give, as they say. And maybe it's right that the ones whose faces seem to be at ten meetings at once are real winners. But would they still be winners if they had to stay home with two broken legs? Are they as good at working the program as they are at talking and sharing about it? The reason I'm wondering is because a fellow mentioned the other night that "anyone can stay sober at an AA meeting—it's the time in between that sorts you out."

Then what about the kind of winner who's going hammer and nails to get onto the committee circuit and into the AA limelight? It's true that we've got to have someone doing the chores but is it also true that we're supposed not really to be "organized as such," and what we're actually supposed to have is "trusted servants" who serve the fellowship and know the spiritual meaning of "rotation." But at the same time it's also possible to get yourself a lot of prestige and importance if you're absolutely determined to serve rather than just being willing if able and asked.

One of the co-founders of AA spelled something out in writing and I came upon it last week, and what he said was this. "In as large an organization as ours, we have our share of schemers for personal gain, petty swindlers, and confidence men." Now I wouldn't argue with what he said because the man was speaking straight truth. But the only thing I'm wondering about is that schemers, swindlers, and confidence men sometimes stay off the sauce for years and stay around the meetings.

So are they winners? I mean, what about the people who cadged and conned and lied and cheated and generally wiped their dirty feet on anyone in sight on their way "up" in sobriety and now sit with a well-oiled bank balance, talking pearly words about the Program? Am I really supposed to stick with and become like this kind of winner?

As I said, I've been looking around and I've been wondering about this "winner" thing. I don't think you can ever possibly become a winner unless you do stay continuously sober, but that still leaves a terrific amount of room for variety and I think I've found the sort of winners I want to stick with. The funny thing is they don't actually hit you in the face as big successes in sobriety. They haven't gone zooming up in the world and they're not big cheeses and somehow they don't very often get elected on to the big high-up committees or asked to speak on the circuit.

It's a bit hard to say just what it is about them that makes them the kind of winners I want to stick with, but in a strange way it's because they're a lot more likely to think of themselves sometimes as losers compared to the "winners." A lot of them seem to have had things like losing jobs and shaky health and terrible disappointments and depressions, all in sobriety. They've stayed sober and tried to learn something from all these negative experiences, and they also seem to laugh a lot of the time. They sit just any old where at the meetings, but you get a nice feeling that something sort of special has happened to them. Once in a while they take the lead at a meeting, if they are asked, but you know that they're just as happy helping with the chairs at the end of the meeting. They do their Twelfth Step work when they get the opportunity but they don't tell the whole of AA they're doing it. They do their stint as a "trusted servant" too when it's their turn and they manage to stay sort of anonymous about it, like weeding a garden.

What makes them the kind of winners I want to stick with is that they're not quite like all the other kinds of winners I've mentioned. They haven't got the big success story, money or jobwise; they've had to survive spells when they couldn't go to meetings and couldn't be in the swim of things; they've got nothing big going for them in the way of prestige—and still they've stayed sober without cheating themselves or other people.

I'll tell you what it comes down to. They are the sober, living spirit of this AA fellowship as I understand it. And, if they look like losers to you, that's okay by me—just so long as you leave me with them.

AAs SHOULD BE HONEST ABOUT SEX PROBLEMS
One Member's Plea For More Widespread Discussion And Understanding Of A Seldom Mentioned Subject In The Recovery Program

Many people who write on the subject of sex problems feel obliged to explain that sex is basically good—that it is God's method of guaranteeing the reproduction of mankind. This startling information is usually supplied defensively, almost as if to combat the grim possibility that sex might be legislated out of existence if somebody doesn't present a worthwhile case for it. The authors, of course, are really pleading for the right to discuss sex difficulties openly. Prudery on the printed page was vanquished a long time ago. But the near-pornography which replaced it is a poor counterfeit of honesty. Truth is still mighty hard to find, and it's even harder to present.

How the outside world wishes to deal with this subject is not really our affair, but it is important that we face the matter more honestly in AA. AA has a number of supplementary pamphlets for employers, wives, and young alcoholics, but none on what is often the most critical problem in our fellowship. Our speakers thunder eloquently about the need for absolute honesty, but only a few hardy souls ever dare to hint that sex might have been a disturbing problem area. An outsider could easily get the impression—judging by what we print and what we say—that alcoholics don't have sex problems at all.

It's a different matter when we turn to the literature published by outside observers. AA members may wish to evade the issue, but others are more objective about it. They point to sexual confusion as a significant factor in the alcoholic's personality disturbances. Sometimes their conclusions seem hastily and unfairly drawn; when, for example, a psychiatrist uses a few representative case histories to prove that almost all alcoholics are afflicted with certain types of sexual abnormality. In general, however, sex facts are included as a matter of course in any scientific inquiry into the subject of alcoholism. And a psychiatrist who treats an alcoholic will most certainly concern himself with the patient's sex history.

However, if we are completely honest about it, we don't even need outside observers to tell us the extent of our sex problems. We are very familiar with the oft-repeated remark, sometimes heard after an older member has resumed drinking, "Well, the poor fellow has 'other' problems." These "other" problems usually have something to so with sex. When you hear a remark like this you don't even have to ask for further details; the emphasis on "other" conveys a world of hidden meanings. Extramarital philandering exists in AA—though probably not on a large scale—and the pretty young woman who joins a group can expect "sponsorship" of a very thorough kind.

The truth is that alcoholics do have unusually troublesome sex problems. It would be almost unbelievable if people plagued by our kind of illness did not have various sex disturbances. We may not like to admit it, just as we did not like to admit our alcoholism. But when we say that "some poor fellow who had 'other' shortcomings resumed drinking," aren't we admitting indirectly that we understand the tremendous pressures of these "other" problems? Aren't we conceding that misdirected sex is a formidable threat to sobriety? Aren't we saying that AA can help a person recover if he isn't tyrannized too severely by sex? And aren't we also saying—by implication, of course—that since we are sober ourselves, we aren't troubled by these problems?

After almost eleven years of continuous sobriety in the AA program, I've found myself growing tired of the evasion and hypocrisy surrounding this subject. I have seen the elder statements af AA frown their disapproval when a more honest member brought up his own sex problems and discussed them with remarkable frankness and humility. I have known AA members who thought it gay and sophisticated to laugh at an off-color joke told by a visiting speaker, but who became uneasy and embarrassed if another visiting speaker explored the relationship of sex and alcoholism. And I have seen far too many older members working overtime trying to prove that absolutely insupportable notion that alcoholics are generally "just normal folks who drank too much, too often, too long."

Evasions and hypocrisy may serve certain individuals adequately, but in the long run we progress according to the amount of truth about ourselves we are able to digest. We achieved sobriety by admitting the truth about our drinking problem, and by applying AA's recommended program of recovery. Do we believe that the truth—which rescued us so effectively in one instance—is somehow pernicious and undesirable if applied to other life problems?

What are these sex problems that defy discussion? Most likely they are a cross-section of the same problems that confront society outside of AA. Many alcoholics feel sexually inadequate, and have always been troubled by fears of sexual incompetence and rejection. Oddly, this may have led to frenzied promiscuity. It may have caused an unsatisfactory sex relationship in marriage. It may also have led to sex conduct that society considers immoral or deviated. In fact, it may lead in any number of directions, but the result is always pain, misery, tension, and guilt.

These are only the beginnings of sorrows for the sex-troubled alcoholics who join AA. Unless they are very fortunate, they won't find much understanding and guidance in this critical problem area. He and she will secretly fear they are sexually "different" from the majority of alcoholics, for their only trouble seems to be that "they drank too much, too often, too long." They will be urged to take the Fifth Step, but will have to search for many a moon to find an understanding ear for all their problems. They may achieve sobriety, but it will have the characteristics of an armed truce rather than a genuine peace development.

Really, there's no excuse for it. Sex problems are powerful and deep-seated, but they need not threaten our eligibility for true sobriety and genuine happiness. There are now many older members who have a remarkable understanding on this subject. They need only to tell the truth, so that newcomers will be encouraged to face the truth themselves. This won't eliminate sex anxiety overnight, but it will be a good start. We cannot guarantee that our AA program of recovery, even with its strong emphasis on personal inventory and spiritual help, will aid all alcoholics in solving the "other" problems that seem to be such a threat to continued sobriety. But it is not unreasonable to believe that a more candid approach may create a reservoir of understanding that we do not presently have.

I am not proposing that our AA meetings should become forums for morbid recitals of lecherous behavior. I am sure that "boudoir-to-boudoir" descriptions would eventually be as boring and pointless as many of the drink-by-drink accounts we now endure. Nor am I suggesting an open flaunting of intimate facts that might better be left to private discussions between individual members. My main plea is for a general climate of open-mindedness when this problem seems to be inviting discussion.

This would fulfill—not destroy—the spirit and principles of Alcoholics Anonymous.[3]

TIME TO STOP BLAMING OURSELVES

When we drank, we blamed everyone except ourselves and alcohol for what befell us. We were victims surrounded by enemies and with only one friend: booze.

Surrender brought us the realization that alcohol had betrayed us constantly and that our actions were solely our responsibilities. But, having accepted the latter point, we need not belabor the subject. Our earliest advice is to forget the past except when we visit it briefly to accent lessons learned from experience.

Yet, all too often, we continue to blame ourselves for old (and new) misdeeds and faulty thinking. Self-blame will not permit the spiritual growth that sobriety requires.

Many in Alcoholics Anonymous refer to finger-pointing, whether inwardly or at others, as blame-throwing. When we blame ourselves, guilt arises. Self-guilt can grow into remorse. The next step can well be a feeling of shame. The least result of shame is a loss of the restored self-esteem we gained in our program. There are not too many more steps toward a return to the bottle for those of us who lose confidence in our own ability.

Strength, of course, comes from coping with our own mistakes. We learn to accept any failure, large or small, as normal for all human beings. We happily remember that there are no saints among us and that we are joyous over spiritual progress since we know that perfection can never become a dream.

When we are self-blamers, it is because we reach stages where we cannot be satisfied with what we have become—even in the fact of knowing what kind of "animals" we had been when drinking. Among the saddest expressions heard from AA members at meetings is the self-appraisal: "I haven't changed a bit in AA. I'm the same lousy so-and-so I was when I came in. Except, I'm sober."

That simply is not true. But it is a perfect hitting of the self-blame target by a blame-thrower.

What many of us forget is that we are in an active, not passive program. When any human, in AA or outside our Fellowship, is "doing things," human nature holds true that there will be errors, time of carelessness, impoliteness, even rudeness. The adage says, "To be human is to err." It doesn't tell us to flog ourselves for not being, and doing, right at all times.

A large part of our tendency to be self-blamers while in recovery often lies in the fact that our ego, subdued in surrender to reality, keeps surfacing to assert itself. How frequently our put-down thinking is accompanied by such thoughts as "I'm too smart to make mistakes like that," or "I've become too nice a person to suddenly become hateful."

There also can be an embarrassing amount of cowardice in our cruel blaming of ourselves. All too often, we are besieged with deep concern that "People are going to stop liking me because of the way I'm acting," or "How can I ever merit trust from anyone again after the things I've done?" Guilt turns many of us into people-pleasers.

Another danger of directing blame inwardly is that we can readily move to indulging in expressions of weakness . . . saying "I did the best I could and it wasn't enough" can move further: "I'll never do any better no matter how hard I try," and "I can't ever make amends." Such conclusions are, of course, self-pity. When we feel unworthy, we are making sure that little of true value can come our way.

The "antidote" is simple: Don't create a feeling of guilt where none exists. Self-acceptance is necessary no matter how we act or think when we commit errors.

Above all, self-forgiveness is vital. Blunders must be analyzed and the answers utilized. Mistakes, once corrected, are excused by us error-committers. If others cannot forgive, that is their problem. We have found the courage to face failure.[9]

DEFINING ENVY

There are at least three things that ought to be said about Envy:

1. How much of our criticism of others is due to unconscious envy? Sometimes we criticize or belittle or even jeer at someone who is successful. We may criticize the methods of such a man or the theology of such a woman. Let a person examine themselves, and let them be sure their criticism is not born of envy. If they find the faintest taint of envy in their heart, let them be silent and forever hold their peace.

2. Envy comes from failing to count our blessings, and failing to realize there is a something we can do extremely well. Remember what the little squirrel said to the great mountain: "I cannot carry forests on my back, but you cannot crack a nut."

3. The root cause of envy is the exaltation of self. So long as we think of our own prestige, our own importance, our own reputation, our own rights, we will necessarily be envious. When we learn to think in terms of responsibilities and not of privileges, envy will die a natural death. When we forget ourselves and think of others, the desire to share and serve will put an end to envy.

SOBRIETY MASK

The question often arises in AA circles as to why "John Doe" got drunk after five years of sobriety. Sometimes the story continues: "He was so active in 'service work,' he was at all the AA functions, he seemed to have it all together," the list goes on and on.

I have studied this question and through my own experience have come up with an answer. DISHONESTY. I have just found myself trapped in a very terrifying situation. Let me explain.

Most of us seem to agree that we hide behind a mask before we came to AA. But since coming to AA many of us formed another mask. The dreaded "sobriety mask." This mask is cunning, baffling, and powerful. While we are behind this mask we deceive others into believing that we "have it all together." But this is where the real danger lies . . . we deceive ourselves into believing the same thing.

What is the solution? One thing this false image can't live with, is truth. I find it helpful to ask myself, "When was the last time I shared what was really going on inside me, in my innermost world, with somebody or with my home group?"

You know, the Big Book says we should share our experience, strength, and hope. But, when behind my mask, I only share my opinions, attitudes, and advice. It's safer . . . or is it?

THERE'S NO DIPLOMA IN AA
I Quit Going To Meetings

I used to hear people say there was no graduation from AA and I was determined to prove them wrong. They said AA was a Way of Life and alcoholics kept going to meetings to learn how to live. My compulsion to drink was gone and I thought I knew how to live. I didn't think I needed meetings any more.

So I quit going and after a while I quit praying. Self came in with all its arrogance and started running my life—and everyone knows how well that went. When I started hurting, I wouldn't tell anyone—they might have suggested I go to a meeting and then my argument about not needing meetings would become invalid. I just withdrew, instead—licked my wounds—took a tranquilizer or smoked a little pot. Oh, I didn't drink but I sure was sick. I remember that things got real rough a couple of times and I asked God for help. He helped me just like He always had. But as soon as things were running smoothly again, I forgot about God and took the director's chair again. And just like always, the actors wouldn't do what I wanted them to do and I got angry and resentful and fearful. And life became unmanageable again. I was financially, emotionally, and spiritually bankrupt and I wasn't even drinking.

I hit bottom—again. And I finally understood that "alcohol was only a symptom" of my illness.

I went back to meetings and learned that I knew nothing—that I was only a baby in the program. But I began to ask for help, listened, and shared with others. I rejoined a group and made new friends and renewed old friendships.

Now AA is a school for me and I don't want to graduate. I want to keep on learning the things I need to live a reasonably contented life—one day at a time. I might be in AA kindergarten now; I'm not sure. I know I have to keep this program real simple—just don't drink, and go to meetings. Who needs meetings? I know I do! How about you?

I CANNOT FIX PEOPLE

The longer I am in AA, the more I realize that all I have to give to another alcoholic is my experience, strength and hope in my recovery from alcoholism.

I am not qualified to be a marital counselor, job counselor, spiritual advisor, or any other type of expert. My "advisory abilities" are limited to how I got sober and how I maintain my sobriety. I cannot fix people.

I have found that everyone has the answers to his problems in his own heart and all I can do is listen and tell my own experiences. Sometimes at meetings, we tend to believe we can fix people. Don't let me get such a big ego as to think I have all the answers and I can play demigod.

I pray that I remember what I am and accept the fact that I am a drunk, who through the Grace of God, does not need to drink today.

MEETINGS ARE NOT A SOMETIME THING

I've noticed that something happens to some of us after the first few years of sobriety. We become dissatisfied. We begin to find fault with the meetings and the people at them. We want more.

We find other things to do with our time. After all, it's been some time since we had to think about not drinking and we reason that we don't need meetings to stay sober.

Besides, after all of my hard work, I deserve a break. With all of this sobriety, isn't it time to be normal?

This line of reasoning should flash **DANGER**, but we have a disease that tells us we're not sick.

It is surely right and good that we should get to the point that we want to do more with sobriety than just go to meetings. I believe that our Higher Power has allowed us sobriety so we can now become active, useful members of society. But left to myself and my disease-thinking I will soon believe again that my answers are **out there**.

No matter how many 24 hours I've been sober, I need to keep coming back to hear the message that my answers come through working the Twelve Steps.

An important point I think we some-timers forget is that we owe our lives to AA. The Grace of God through the Fellowship of AA has blessed me with the option to live and join the human race. I can begin to give back a little of what was given to me by doing my share to make sure the meetings are there for the next suffering alcoholic. By passing on what was given to me, others can have the option to live.

If I'm not at the meeting that process can't occur and then, I believe, we are all at risk. Let's not cheat ourselves and the Fellowship in pursuit of some delusion we call a "normal" life. We have a disease that progresses even as we recover, so I doubt we can ever truly be "normal."

If we are having trouble accepting that, then it's back to Step One and more meetings.

Isn't that what we'd tell the newcomer?[36]

ARE YOU RELUCTANTLY, PASSIVELY, HAPPILY, OR JOYOUSLY SOBER?

All member of Alcoholics Anonymous who are honest with themselves are sober. Some are reluctantly sober. Others are passively sober. Some are happily sober. Others are joyously sober. Why is there a difference? It's the quality of their sobriety. Sober is sober, you may say. If a guy or the gal isn't drinking then he's sober. If he or she is drinking then he or she isn't sober. That's all there is to it. But that isn't all there is to it. A ride on the water wagon will bring sobriety, at least for the duration of the ride. But it's likely to be a pretty low grade of sobriety. It's a reluctant sobriety, the I-don't-like-this-but-I've-got-to kind. The rider is so sorry for himself he won't even talk to the driver. He might just as well be going through a tunnel for all the passing scene means to him. Some members of AA are like that.

Then there's the passive sobriety. This alcoholic has reached the bottom below which he doesn't want to go, so he joins AA. He comes to meetings, listens a bit, talks a bit, puts enough of the principles to work to keep himself sober, takes only a passive interest in the group, seldom has time for Twelfth Step work, absorbs as much as he needs and gives only what is brushed from him through contact. He's sober, yes. But he isn't the kind of member that has made AA grow, that has enabled AA to reach out to the thousands of hopeless drunks and restore them to sanity. He isn't particularly happy or unhappy. He's rather numb about the whole thing. Fortunately, there aren't too many members like him.

Then there's the happy type of sobriety. This fellow

accepts his defeat that he and liquor don't get along—and takes hold of AA with enthusiasm. He seems to grasp the program quickly and shows that he's putting it to work. He enters into group affairs and carries his share or more than his share of the load. He attends meetings. He does Twelfth Step work as it comes and hunts for more. He tends to be a little evangelistic at the start, later cools off as he gains experience, and becomes a solid member of the group. He's pretty happy about the whole thing. He's changed his pattern of life and his associations. And while occasionally he may long momentarily for the good old days when liquor was fun—before it became a problem to him —he doesn't brood about it and he's fairly well satisfied with his lot. Many members stay in this class through their association with the fellowship. But a great many more stay in this group only for while, then slip almost unnoticed into another classification.

This last is the group which enjoys a joyous sobriety. Those who are blessed with joyous sobriety can't be separated physically from the happily sober ones. No halo hangs over their heads. No particular gleam sparkles from their eyes. Theirs is an inward joyousness that stems from gratitude to a gracious God who has selected them from the great mass of alcoholics for special consideration, a God who might have picked any one of thousands of hopeless drunks but instead elected to present them with the gift of sobriety. These joyous AAs are humble folk who know that humility consists not in groveling but in having a true perspective of their spiritual assets and liabilities. These are the members to whom others refer as having achieved serenity, although they'd be the first to deny it. Their lives aren't serene, but they have achieved the ability to take things as they come, to roll with the punches, to change those things they can, and to ask the God of their understanding for guidance and counsel in all things.

These are the folks who started doing for others because they were told they should, that it was a part of the program. But as they grew spiritually they found that in direct proportion to the amount of good they did willingly and freely, with no thought of recompense, the good things of life both spiritually and materially were returned to them. Soon they needed no reason for doing good. They now just do it as a part of decent living. They live a day at a time, place themselves in the hands of a Higher Power each morning to carry out His will for that day, ask daily to be so filled with His grace that it can be passed on to others. In doing these things they don't think of themselves as anything special. They do only what they think in their hearts they should. We all know them. While they give no outward indication they stand out everywhere. They're the rocks with which the temple of AA has slowly risen. We can all be like them if only we will put forth the effort. It is up to us.[37]

THE ALCOHOLIC'S WORST ENEMY
Rationalization

Alcoholics are masters at rationalization, which is nothing more than the science of arranging to do what we want to do, then making it appear reasonable. Rationalization is probably the greatest enemy of the alcoholic. It plagues him before he gets into AA and often after he arrives; it is a mental process that consigns him to his own private hell of worry and frustration, of fear and loneliness. Alcoholic rationalization is a built-in antidote to recovery. It is the process of illogical reasoning employed by the alcoholic to justify unreasonable behavior and attitudes in a (for him) reasonable manner.

From the first troublesome drink, this fantastic process is evident. His startled dismay at the adverse results of drinking cause him to blame anything and everything but the real culprit . . . alcohol. If the alcoholic applied logic to the situations, alcoholism would never get beyond the discovery stage. **Problem**: When I drink, I get into trouble. **Solution**: Don't drink. It would be that simple. However, at this point logic is seldom applied, because the ego is shattered by what the alcoholic feels is a humiliating discovery. His inability to handle booze reflects on his manhood and the quality of his worth as a person. So he convinces himself that if he refuses to admit to the facts it will disappear.

It is at this point that the alcoholic rationalization begins. Distorting the facts and unwilling to accept his inability to learn, he must justify his decision. Reason won't do it. So he isolates himself in a world of self-pity, defiance, frustration, and anger. He becomes totally self-centered, hypersensitive to criticism or suggestion, resenting intensely any interference with his God-given right to drink. Obviously the only thing that would induce any to deliberately continue using alcohol—having complete awareness of its destructive qualities for him is perverted thinking, alcohol rationalization.

And just as obvious is the only possible solution, a complete reversal of this kind of thinking. Because it is so ingrained in many of us, our talent for rationalization does not necessarily leave us when we sober up. We simply divert that talent to other areas of our lives. Constant contact with a solid sponsor is a great way of holding rationalization in check.

IT'S WHAT HAPPENS
IN BETWEEN MEETINGS

Sure the meetings are important. Sure, reading the Big Book is important. Sure, getting a sponsor is important.

But, what the old-timers told me was that most important of all is how I live in between the meetings. They said it's easy to be a nice guy at meetings but how do I act at home? How do I treat my wife and kids? How do I act at work?

They said the spiritual life is no theory; I have to live it. And that means practicing the principles of AA in all my affairs.

What an order! I don't know if I can go thru with it. But, fortunately the old-timers added that Step Twelve says we try to practice the principles in all our affairs, which leaves me a loophole. All I have to do then, is try and leave the results up to my Higher Power.

These old-timers insisted that even though I feel much better when I go to a meeting, this is not enough. Sobriety, they said, had very little to do with feelings. They said action is the magic word and the action that really counts takes place between meetings.

They said the Twelve Steps are a plan for living, not just for discussion. They suggested I learn to walk the walk, not just talk the talk.

Only by trying to carry the message and trying to practice the principles can I grow in sobriety and enjoy the Promises.

Like a juicy cheeseburger, it's what's in between that counts!

STEP SEVEN
Humbly Asked Him To Remove Our Shortcomings

Humbly asked who? To remove what? Shortcomings? What are they? It seems as long as I kept asking these questions, even after getting many answers from my sponsor, Big Book, friends in AA, etc., I didn't have to "take" this step. It's like asking the question "Why?" Why is the unanswerable question for me. Just like a little child when they ask "why?" When they get the answer, they ask "why?" again and again and so on. I used the question like a hold-off on Step Seven.

The fact is that when I took this Step on one of my short-comings—false pride—it gave me the opening I needed to continue to use thisSstep as another "self-knowledge" step (like Four, Five and Six). Step Seven has the power of disconnecting from "old self." Certainly, I have admitted my powerlessness, unmanageability, dishonesties, and childlike behavior, but they had become so much a part of me that I felt threatened to have these things removed. In fact, I considered my over-reacting as a part of me that was useful or at least it was "just me" and people would have to learn to accept that about me.

It's funny now, but as I received the knowledge of self, I realized that I had created the Dave S. Construction Company, and my specialty was walls. In a wink of an eye, I had walls erected that could keep out anyone, anything—even God. I had to file a "bankruptcy" notice and go through the process of surrendering all of my shortcomings in order for me to get on to living without the safety of my old shortcomings. Certainly, I have still got some, but they are usually located in my "pride locker"; and when I am capable of an honest, humble reawakening, I will report my status to myself, my squad, or AA friends. Of course, it is impossible for me to do that without giving it to my Higher Power.

So, I stop building walls, make decisions, and act as if I want to be happy, serene, sane, and go on trying to carry the message of spiritual awakenings. Knowing now that the best way to stay away from removing my own shortcomings is to accentuate my good characteristics and be honest about what is really a human limitation, not a character defect. To keep uppermost in my mind and heart that all of those things that keep me from God stem from pride, mental laziness, dishonesty, and procrastination. Thank God He is working on them now. If He wasn't, I would not have written this.[27]

THE PROPER SPIRIT
Our Selfish Program

Most of us that have attended meetings with some regularity have heard this familiar statement repeated many times at AA meetings: "This is a selfish program," which is partially true. However, to the new person, it is confusing and particularly so when he sees his AA friends giving so much without asking for anything in return.

What really makes this so-called selfish program difficult to explain to the new person is when he hears his AA friends talk about the midnight telephone calls, the Twelve Step calls, the one hundred mile round trip to speak at another AA meeting and the five dollar bill passed to someone under the table, who is in need. What makes it more confusing is that the people who are sharing with others, seem to get a sense of satisfaction every time they go out and help another human being.

In our drinking days, most of us were great sharers as long as it was the other fellow's share. Some of us had to depend on others to share with us because we didn't have anything to support our drinking habit. We added up every penny and nickel to see if we had enough to buy a cheap bottle of wine and if we didn't, we would beg or steal, for many of us came into AA with the habit of counting pennies and nickels. Some of us became so conservative with our money that we palmed our dime and dropped it silently in the basket and it looked strange among the dollars and the sight of that dime gave us a feeling of guilt.

As we continued going to meetings and watched our AA friends contributing generously to every AA cause, our dimes gradually became quarters, eventually half-dollars and finally dollars. Today we can look back over the past and see how the AA principles are working, and how our association with our AA friends was actually the thing which broke the chain of our selfish attitude and opened the door to a sober and better life.

Perhaps the real reason why our selfish program is difficult to explain is because it has to be lived, and as we live it a day at a time, the mystery of our AA principles unfold, slowly and surely, and gradually we begin to understand that it is in sharing that we receive. In the measure in which we share with others, our own burdens become lighter. In the measuring up to life's demands our character will grow to widening sympathy and deeper understanding. There is no question to the meaning of sharing with others. Every time we share with another human being, we add something to our spiritual and moral bank account, enabling us to draw on our spiritual savings account when extra demands are made upon our moral courage. During an emergency is not the time to start our bank account as it must be in the bank when we need it.

Yes, this is a selfish program and perhaps it will never change, but we must change our attitude of grabbing for ourselves, to the spirit of sharing with others. This is the spirit we need to carry the message to another sick alcoholic, this is the spirit which helps the General Service Office and the *Grapevine* to operate; this is the spirit which keeps the hand of AA always there, when anyone, anywhere, reaches out for help, this is the spirit of responsibility.[16]

VI. THE REVEREND CANON SAMUEL M. SHOEMAKER

THE MEANING OF SELF-SURRENDER
The Reverend Canon Samuel M. Shoemaker
1928

The meaning of self-surrender to God is the deepest meaning in all the experience of religion. There is something deep-hidden within us which makes us feel that whatever God is, He is more ideal than we are, and that we shall tend to find our life by yielding it, in as nearly an absolute sense as possible, to the Ideal Power which we call God. The very earliest stirrings of faith in God carry with them some natural response of this sort. It is hard for us to think of God without thinking also of our duty towards Him, and it is impossible to conceive that duty in any vitally personal sense without the consciousness that we cannot begin to do it until we have first offered the whole of ourselves to God. Like human love, religion is impossible without the maximum of self-giving.

I am perfectly sure that self-surrender is for most people an unrealized aspiration. They feel the edges of it in great moments of joy or of sadness. Music stirs it in them, if they are susceptible to music. Art may do it, or a sunset sky. A great spoken word, or the convincing life of a saint—there are a thousand possible stimuli to the thought of self-surrender to the Power of the universe. But this generally goes off into diffuse ether. The thing is mostly emotion which does not harness itself to something that needs to be done. It is fitful and unsustained. It is a glimpse we get into reality, that does not last long enough to become an abiding possession, a permanent attitude of obedience and trust and loving co-operation.

If I can today, I want to draw this thing out of the vague region where for most of us it resides, only occasionally invading our minds, and put it where it may become actual for us all. May I say to you, frankly and personally, that I was a missionary on foreign soil, with a Christian home, confirmation, many student conferences, and a decision to enter the ministry behind me, before I ever saw the luminous depths, the liberating power, of the experience of self-surrender? My brethren, these things ought not so to be; and it is one of the great resolves of my ministry that they shall not be where, by preaching and talking in season and out of season, upon the reality of the experience, I can prevent them from being. It is a lamentable thing that in our religious instruction, and our preaching, we can hit upon so many peripheral and secondary things, while Christian people go through their lives without knowing that this central experience is possible for them.

William James has told us that people belong to one of two types, the once-born, or the twice-born type. Emerson was a type of the first, a mind always at unity with itself, with little consciousness of duality or division, which holds communion with the Absolute as with a familiar Friend, and which finds harmony and peace by falling naturally into step with the purposes of Providence. The twice-born type is aware of disunity, division, a rift at the center of being, something in oneself that is out of gear and out of step and needs righting. St. Paul is the archetype of it, and the heart of the need for second birth is his cry: "Wretched man that I am! Who shall deliver me from the body of death?" The once-born type takes naturally to goodness and elevated activity which makes for happiness and peace. The twice-born type is beset with anxieties and inward friction which can only find happy activity after an inward readjustment has taken place.

A great many of us belong to the twice-born group, or ought to belong to it, who need to find it out. We like to think we are once-born, and all right as we are. We have glossed over the division and disunity within us by a fictitious outward self-possession and quietness. But the rift can only be fully healed when we have given ourselves over to God.

Now, for this twice-born type, there are two possible ways of surrendering. A surrender may be largely a deliberate act of will. A man having seen the issue of surrender, and knowing that God wants the whole of his life unreservedly, may make the plunge and throw himself utterly upon God to do with as He will. Such a surrender is that described by Prof. Henry B. Wright, of Yale, when he says of a meeting he attended at Northfield: "I was afraid I should be asked to go as a foreign missionary, but I went down. There, seated in an armchair at one end of the room, was the greatest human I have ever known, Dwight L. Moody. He spoke to us simply and briefly about the issues of life, using John 7:17 as his theme: 'If any man willeth to do his will, he shall know of the teaching, whether it be of God, or whether I speak from myself.' There in the quiet, without anyone knowing what was going on, I gave myself to God, my whole mind, heart and body: and I meant it." Those of you who know of Henry Wright's profound influence for more than twenty years upon student life in this country, and the emphasis he always put on the need for absolute surrender to God's will, will not ask whether such an experience is lasting; you will know that it is both lasting and widely multiplying.

I could give you a hundred instances of men and women whom I have known, who have, at a critical place in their lives, made this momentous turning and have never retraced their steps or gone back on their decision. You may be the kind of person who, having seen the choice, must deliberately, coolly, sanely, and with resolve, hand yourself to God by making a deed of trust for your life, disposing of yourself to Him so that you can never take yourself back again.

There are others of this twice-born type who cannot thus take the kingdom of heaven by force. There are two elements in the complete experience of which I speak, if surrender grows into conversion: man's turn, and God's search. For some of us, the critical element is the dedication of our own wills. For others it is the moment of God's invasion. Surrender is, then, not so much effort as is required in throwing ourselves over upon the mercy of God, but only so much effort as is needed to open the door of our life to Him. We must all know that what God does for us in a conversion is the great matter, and not what we do for ourselves: but there are natures in which this is the supreme part, in the sense that surrender is a passive thing rather than an active one. I am not now talking about resignation under pain and trouble, which is quite another question. I am speaking of the need for an open and relaxed and unstruggling mind as the medium through which God can alone come into the lives of some people. Possibly there is an element of each emphasis needed in us all, so that we both make the effort of deliberate self-surrender and also cease from all effort, so that no exertion on our part may interfere with God's dealing with us. We may not be able to tell which is to be our particular means of surrendering until we try it.

One is bound to be asked the question whether it is a relatively sudden matter for many, and a combination of suddenness and gradualness for others. For the person who wakes up to the fact that they are matured in every other way, but babes in their spiritual development, so that the great experience of religion has yet to come, I believe that it is likely to be an experience which takes place at a definite and recognized time. It is significant that James wrote: "Self-surrender has been and always must be regarded as the vital turning-point of the religious life . . . One may say that the development of Christianity in inwardness has consisted in little more than the greater and greater emphasis attached to this crisis of self-surrender." Crisis, mark you, not process.

The process which comes before the act of surrender is the long discovery that the way of self is no way at all, and leads nowhither—the lonely, despairing, feverish desire to be rid of oneself. And the process which comes after the act of surrender is the steady matching-up of the actual with the ideal, the rethinking and remoulding life in accordance with the great decision. Both processes may take time, much time. But the decision itself has the definiteness about it which any decision has: you may prepare long for a decision, you may work long to carry it out. But when you decide, the hammer falls, and there cannot be delay.

Now I want to speak of four immediate results of surrender, when one has wholly let go of one's life, and is living continually with reference to God. By these I think it fair to test whether we have surrendered or not.

The first is a wide sense of liberation. The queer thing about self-will is that it kills the very thing it wants: freedom. If you know any more abject slave than the man or woman who has throughout his life had his own way, I would like to know where you find one. One of my friends tells me, when I talk to him along these lines: "I feel as if you were trying to put a big, black overcoat on me, and button it tight." But it is precisely his own complete control of the issues of his life which is, year after year, buttoning the overcoat tighter and tighter; and it is the very surrender which he fears that alone can bring him liberty. There is no freedom under God's wide heaven like the freedom of having committed yourself, lock, stock, and barrel, to the will of God. The joy of it is an unearthly thing, which follows you and grows greater with the years.

The next result is an enquiry into one's life-plans in the large, to see if they be such as God would choose as His first, best plan for us. For younger people this is bound to concern their life-work and their marriage, and to demand that these great choices be made upon the basis of honest search for God's will. There are in the world a great many empty places, hard places, thrilling places which the world cannot see as thrilling. God wants workers there. There is a lot He wants done in this world, and there are very few who will lay themselves open to His plan, and promise to fit in wherever He says. Here, again, many a man or woman fears he must become a missionary, or give up what promises to be a successful worldly marriage to wait for one with better foundations; and it seems a heavy cross. Yet when one makes the commitment with regard to these large life-plans, he finds that God makes no mistakes, and the thing he thought he could never do may be the very thing he loves to do most.

There is a retroactive element in a genuine surrender, too. You cannot give your life to God without being willing to turn back into the past, and there make right the things you know to have been wrong. Past wrong leaves its roots in our subconscious minds, and if you dig below the soil you will find the old foundations just as they were left. Personal relationships which have been filled with misunderstandings and irritation, business deals which have compromised principle, injustice which calls for the fairness to reopen the question, rudeness or criticism or tale-bearing which only honest apology and confession will make right—these things feel the change in the atmosphere when we have genuinely surrendered, and they must be acclimatized to the new life. Nobody has really given in to God who leaves untouched the unforgiven grudge, or the unrighted wrong. The new life demands a clean slate.

And then there must be growing victory over sin. Deliverance!—that was the cry of victory of Christianity to the first century. St. Paul went into a rotten port-city like Corinth, infested with all the degradation of the worst of Greek degeneracy, and told his people he was determined to know nothing among them but Jesus Christ. Real Christianity has always been able to save men from sin. And when I find people who have all their lives been coming to church, and have never mastered a quick tongue, a disagreeable spirit, the touchiness which resents the slightest interference with one's own desires, and which makes one hard to get along with, I do not say the Christianity has failed, I say that we Christians have simply not surrendered our whole hearts to the Lord Jesus Christ.

For two nights of this past week my work has carried me to the Jerry McAuley Water Street Mission. I heard there the vivid and simple and unostentatious testimonies of men who had been redeemed from all kinds of sin. They said they had been kept for two days, several weeks, twenty years, by the power of Christ. There is a difference between that happy and vivid and unashamed religion, and our decent and reticent and less effective kind: the difference isn't in the amount of decency nearly so much as it is in the amount of power. I would to God the churches of this city had in them the power that is there, that we expected people to be converted as they do, expected them to witness as they do. And back of that power over broken sin there lies a great yielding, a deep surrender to the love and will of God.

Now, my friends, I always want to say a special word in a sermon like this to those whose major choices have been made, and who feel it is now a question of making the best of it because it is too late to change. It is never too late. When you miss God's first best plan for you, He has a second, and if you miss that, a third. Your situation is always new to God. He can and will always begin over again to deal with you, and give you another chance. It is a great thing to surrender to God in the fullness of youth, but it is also a great thing to surrender at any time. I beg you not to think of yourselves as too far along the way to change.

Let us today ask ourselves with complete candor whether we ever have surrendered everything to His will. Did we miss His whole plan for us years ago by taking a turn we knew was wrong?

Have we felt the pressure of His love all these years, and feared to respond to it, as Francis Thompson did, "lest having Him, I should have naught beside"?

Have we given Him our homes, our money, our ambition, our joy, our suffering, our human ties, our characters, our hearts? Is there somewhere a conscious withholding?—for if there is, there is so much less of that freedom and joy and peace in believing which comes alone when we give all.

It is one of the dearest hopes of my life that this congregation will learn the art of winning lives to Jesus Christ: the beginning is with ourselves. No man can give what he does not possess. You cannot ask another to give himself to Christ till you have given yourself. This is no academic self-examination. Something is desperately wrong with our modern version of Christianity, and I suspect that it is the want of just this surrender amongst us. I believe you are in or out. Henry Wright startled some people once by saying: "No man or woman oozes unconsciously into the kingdom of God. In the final analysis, all enlist, and every soldier knows when he enlisted." But I believe he was right. Have you ever enlisted? Or have you all your life hung around the recruiting station, and thought about it? God has a place for you, a work for you to do. You will do it, or it will go undone.

"Who then offereth willingly to consecrate himself this day unto Jehovah?"

Let us pray:

O God our Father, it is so easy for us to drift along, and say our prayers and sing our worship as though with all our hearts we loved to do Thy will. Thou knowest us better than we know ourselves, and in Thy presence we see how much of our life is outside Thy control. Grant us grace to give Thee everything we have and are, and use us for Thy glory. For the sake of Jesus Christ our Lord. Amen.[18]

"ACT AS IF—"
The First Step Toward Faith
The Reverend Canon Samuel M. Shoemaker
1954

Some years ago I found myself talking with a congenital skeptic. He had made a fortune and lost it, made another and lost that. Now, he told me, he couldn't pay his rent, and was taking pills in order to sleep. I think he doubted that there was any way out of his predicament.

"Want to try an experiment?" I asked.

He answered, "I don't even believe in God, you know."

"Well," I said, "there is something that seems to help people who do. And I believe that Something will help you if you will let It."

"How can I let It if I don't even believe in It ?" he asked.

I said, "Suppose we try telling the truth about your situation, and the way you feel about it, to whatever is the ultimate Truth and Reality in this universe—and honestly ask that Power for help and guidance."

"How would you do that?" he asked.

I suggested that we kneel down out of reverence toward the Unknown, and then that he say exactly what he felt—not pretending anything he didn't believe but exposing himself to whatever creative force runs through existence.

"Well," he mused, "I certainly am in a jam. I'll try anything once."

He got down on his knees, half laughing at himself, and said, "O God, if there be a God, send me help now, because I need it."

It was a good, honest, selfish prayer. Climbing back into his chair somewhat sheepishly, he said, "I don't feel any different." I told him that I didn't especially care how he felt but I was interested in what he was going to do. I suggested that he read a chapter in the Bible that night before he went to bed—perhaps the third chapter of St. John; and another when he woke up next day—maybe the 12th chapter of St. Luke. I suggested that he come to church Sunday and see whether he could catch anything from the faith of other people. I also suggested that he keep praying. "Keep saying whatever is honest about yourself and your situation to whatever is the Truth behind all creation. I think you'll feel you are being answered."

He tried it—intermittently at first, fighting almost every step of the way. But he kept on with the experiment—his need prodded him. The faith of other people gave him a helpful atmosphere. At last he had to admit that *something* was helping him, for he began sleeping without barbiturates, and his business slowly began to come back.

The skeptic was baptized and confirmed, and later became a vestryman of my church.

How did this man "get religion"? *By acting as if he had faith*—until, indeed, there was an opening for God to come through. Faith is primarily a kind of expectant loyalty toward God, life and the universe, and only secondarily an intellectual conviction. It is much more like falling in love than like adopting a philosophy.

In its earlier stages, the finding of faith may be much like a scientific experiment. You take a hypothesis, test it, confirm or disprove it. Science and religion can be quite close in the important matter of approach. As James Russell Lowell phrased it, "Science was faith once."

Some will say, "But isn't it hypocrisy to 'act as if' when you really don't believe at all?" My answer is that it is not hypocrisy for a scientist to regard a hypothesis as true long enough to prove that it is or is not. A real experiment, entered into with an honest and open mind, is an avenue to truth.

One day a young doctor with a warm heart, who was experiencing the tragedy of pain and illness in children for the first time, met a minister whom he knew and said, "I guess I need to talk to you. Instead of believing more in God, sometimes I feel like shaking my fist in His face and saying, 'Damn you for letting little children suffer like this!'"

Instead of being shocked, the minister said, "Probably that is the first real prayer you ever said."

The young doctor was surprised the clergyman would liken what sounded like pure blasphemy to prayer. He was told that if he would pursue this further, and really tell God all that he was thinking and feeling—say *to* God whatever he had felt like saying *about* Him—it might be the first step in an experiment of faith.

It was also suggested to the doctor that prayer is a two-way proposition. After talking to God, why not listen to Him a little while? The doctor did. No great illumination came—only a strong conviction that his job was to alleviate as much pain and suffering as he could, and that somehow God was interested in that. This experimental approach afforded him an avenue to faith.

I watched some ideas of experimental faith being tried out by a group of young married people in Pittsburgh. These people began by acknowledging the fact that Christianity had a primary place in the emergence of our Western ways of freedom and democracy. They went on to ask, "How do you find this faith?"

I pointed out that what we call faith is as evident and real a power in this universe as the power of electricity or the atom, but that samples of faith do far more good than sales talks about it. So these couples began praying to find God's will, not trying to get Him to change it in favor of their own. They put unselfish prayer, love, and faith to work in daily business situations.

One of the young men said to me: "For years I tried to find God by reason and logic. I could find reasons for believing in God, but I could also find reasons for not believing. Then someone told me to act as if God *were*, and see what would happen. I did—and prayer has become a real, life-giving force to me. I live under less pressure, sleep better, make sounder decisions in business, give more time to my family, and am generally a much happier and, I hope, more useful member of society."

He joined the church, took up teaching a class of boys on Sunday, and found a new source of inner power. None of this came by swallowing something he could not digest intellectually, but by exploring in a field where he did not know exploration was possible.

The leap of faith is not the admission of credulity but of a kind of courage. We really believe only when we have found sufficient evidence. The first steps of faith consist of looking for the evidence. And the greatest evidence of all is a firsthand experience of God. That is why we must seek to come into His presence.

So long as we merely talk *about* God, we can indulge a great deal of doubt. But when we walk right into His presence, and talk *to* Him, doubt comes to seem curiously out of place, irrational, silly. I'll wager that what you will get back from Him will not be a blinding light or a gush of sentimental feeling but rather a sense of added strength, some insight about a problem or a person, a realization that you are in touch with more Power than ever before in your life.

In faith, as in every other experiment, there is a point where the experiment turns into an experience. You want to learn to swim. You get in the water and splash around. Somebody tells you what to do with your arms and legs. After a while you find that the water, plus your own efforts, is holding you up and moving you forward.

It is the same with faith. Mrs. Thomas A. Edison told me that her husband worked for five years to create the electric-light bulb. He had faith that such a thing could be made, and had ideas about how it might be done. He tried one way after another until he struck the right one. The world takes the incandescent bulb for granted, but it was one man's faith plus years of trial and error that led to the discovery. Should we begrudge the hours or months or years it may take us to find God?

We need not expect that all hidden meanings will become immediately clear if we make the experimental approach to religion. But we can, as Thomas Huxley enjoins us, exhibit the true scientific spirit by sitting down before the facts as a little child, prepared to give up our preconceived notions.

We need merely to start on our way, and remember the truth of the ancient Chinese proverb: the longest journey begins with a single step.[19]

VII. WILLIAM DUNCAN SILKWORTH, M.D.

PSYCHOLOGICAL REHABILITATION
OF ALCOHOLICS
William D. Silkworth, M.D. 1939

In a study of carefully recorded histories of alcoholics in our hospital, two important facts appear to be outstanding. Expressed briefly, they are:

1. A majority of our patients do not wish to have an alcoholic problem. They lead busy lives and would like to enjoy the fruits of their efforts, but they cannot stop the use of alcohol.

2. These patients cannot use alcohol in moderation.

The allergic nature of true alcoholism was postulated in a previous paper. We then endeavored to show that alcohol does not become a problem to every person who uses it, and that the use of alcohol in itself does not produce a chronic alcoholic.

The phenomenon of craving must be present as a manifestation of an allergy. Once established in an individual, one drink creates a desire for more. It sets this person aside as a separate entity. It creates a conflict which ends in a form of neurosis.

Looking further at the record of these unfortunates, we find that the majority could not drink in moderation from the very beginning. Whether twenty, thirty, or fifty years of age, they soon become a problem to themselves and to their friends.

Now in analyzing these alcoholic-minded persons, there is no one physical or psychical fact that is sufficiently constant to justify its use as the basis of an accepted theory. Such phrases as "escape from reality" and "inferiority complex" hold true for some, but not all, while heredity, only son, and implied spoiling in childhood, account for a few more. They all lead to confusion and have no answer.

Eliminate the constitutional psychopaths, the moral and mental defectives, and there remains a large class, neurotic in type, for whom something is worth doing. Remember we are discussing the chronic alcoholic, not the man who drinks more than is good for him but has no resulting problem.

Apparently all these people—good, bad and indifferent—have one thing in common: they cannot drink in moderation. We believe they show manifestations of an allergy to alcohol. They may abstain from the use of alcohol for a month or a year, but on taking it again in any form, they at once establish the phenomenon of craving. This fact is well known to all alcoholics and creates their major problems in the early stages of their drinking habits. They complain about it, too.

Why, we naturally ask, in the early years of drinking, while they still have the ability to choose, do these people not solve this problem by the complete discontinuance of alcohol? Some do, but many are like the rest of us who do things we know we should not, but like to do them anyway. Many really believe they can drink as they see others doing, and enjoy themselves. For many reasons, most of which are social or even physical, the idea of drinking is developed gradually. As this idea advances, daily life becomes more insecure, but these men are unwilling to accept the facts as presented to them. The act of drinking (in the end damaging) is followed by certain comfortable emotional states which make it a pleasure. They prove to themselves that they can stop drinking by going on the wagon for varying periods, but even as life becomes more complicated, they still persist in that old, original idea. Up to this time, in what one might call the first period of alcoholism there are methods employed to help these persons return to a normal life and accept the fact that their old idea of drinking must be discarded forever. We ourselves have treated some of them with permanent results, but the majority continue along the primrose path. The history of these people and their families present from now on, one of the real tragedies of human life and is too well known to comment on further here.

This begins the second stage. Understood by no one and not understanding themselves, they enter an ever-widening circle, remorse, penance, new transgressions, new penance, until they lose all capacity for spontaneous action. They sacrifice themselves for a perversive idea and defying the law of nature (allergy) operating in their case, pay the penalty. They have lost all pleasure in normal life. Based on their underlying neurotic nature, they develop a compulsion type of thinking, and, although not a true compulsion neurosis, it is surely a border-line type. The patient now acts under what has been called by Wechsler a psychic imperative, the *dreaded terminal state of paralysis of the will*. The predisposing factor in bringing about this definite state of insecurity is the conflict brought about by alcoholism.

It is not within the scope of this paper to discuss the complications of the obsessional neuroses, which are, in fact, the most elastic of all the neuroses, but in this particular type it seems to permit a retreat from the ever increasing anxieties induced by the advancing chronic alcoholism.

This compulsive thinking is apparently a purely intellectual process occurring more frequently among persons of relatively higher intellectual attainment, from which class, by the way, comes the average chronic alcoholic.

Characteristic of all compulsion types of thinking is the relatively good insight which accompanies them. The victim knows his impulse to drink is wrong but he is helpless before it. Wives may plead, friends argue, and employers threaten, but he is no longer amenable to impression. He is unable to resolve between opposing impulses. He cries out in agony, "I must stop, I cannot be like this; but I cannot stop; someone must help me."

If he has sufficient means, he has by now been treated by psychiatrists, good men, who fully realize the unfavorable prognosis, but who, often without remuneration, give freely of their time to help the victim. I have often seen psychoanalysis of an alcoholic, instead of breaking up the compulsive thinking, start the person further theorizing on his own illness.

We know that, as a rule, the only relief from psychoanalysis is in making the so-called transfer, and experience has taught us that this is gratifyingly successful if accomplished. If successful, it must be based on respect and confidence on the part of the patient. It can seldom be accomplished in this class of patients except by one who has suffered in the same manner and has recovered. In other words, to accomplish the transfer of this compulsive idea by the plan we have seen developed, an ex-alcoholic who has recovered by the same means must be the medium employed. Such a medium can explain convincingly, not only that the transfer of the compulsive thinking can be made, but he can prove how he did it himself successfully.

We physicians have realized for a long time that some form of moral psychology was of urgent importance to alcoholics, but its application presented difficulties beyond our conception. What with our ultramodern standards, our scientific approach to everything, we are perhaps not well equipped to apply the powers of good lying outside our synthetic knowledge.

About four years ago, a young man was hospitalized by us for severe chronic alcoholism, and, while under our care he developed a plan which seemed to me to be a combination of psychology and religion. He never drank any form of alcohol again.

Later he requested the privilege of being allowed to tell his story to other patients and, perhaps with some misgiving, we consented. The cases we have followed through have been most interesting: in fact many of them are amazing. The unselfishness of these men as we have come to know them, the entire absence of profit motive and their community spirit, are indeed inspiring to one who has labored long and wearily in the field of alcoholism. They believe in themselves, and still more in the Power which pulls chronic alcoholics back from the gates of death.

Of course, prior to and in preparation for the application of this plan, it is, in my opinion, essential to detoxicate the alcoholics by hospitalization. You then have a subject whose brain is clear and whose mind is receptive and temporarily free from his craving. I hesitate here to attempt even an outline of the plan as employed by these men. Sufficient to say, perhaps, that following many failures, they gradually devised a plan or procedure which led them to make this so-called transfer to one greater than themselves, to God.

The whole story is admirably told in a book written by them entitled *Alcoholics Anonymous.* It would seem to me that they have wrung from the Eternal a new application of an old truth which is sufficient equipment to restore the patient in his fight for sobriety. The results seem to flow naturally from a follow-up of honest effort.

To make any such plan practical they have also projected this transfer beyond the individual to the group. The formation of these men into groups, each one with the hand of fellowship passing on his experiences to others, helping those who have newly joined to adjust themselves, actively engaged in gathering in new members, seems to me the most practical application of their moral psychology, to assure their "transfer" of being permanent. (Altogether I have met some thirty or more of these ex-alcoholics. I relate my experience with two of them.)

About one year prior to this experience a man was brought in to be treated for chronic alcoholism. He had but partially recovered from a gastric hemorrhage and seemed to be a case of pathological mental deterioration. He had lost everything worth while in life, and was only living, one might say, to drink. He frankly admitted and believed that for him there was no hope. Following the elimination of alcohol there was found to be no permanent brain injury. He accepted the plan outlined in the book. One year later he called to see me, and I experienced a very strange sensation. I knew the man by name and partly recognized his features, but there all resemblance ended. From a trembling, despairing, nervous wreck, had emerged a man brimming over with self-reliance and contentment. I talked with him for some time, but was not able to bring myself to feel that I had known him before. To me he was a stranger, and so he left me. More than three years have now passed with no return to alcohol.

When I need a mental uplift, I often think of another case brought in by a physician, prominent in New York City. The patient had made his own diagnosis, and deciding that his condition was hopeless, had hidden in a deserted barn, determined to die. He was rescued by a searching party, and in desperate condition brought to me. Following his physical rehabilitation, he had a talk with me in which he frankly stated he thought the treatment a waste of time and effort, unless I could assure him, which no one ever had, that in the future he could have the will power to resist the impulse to drink. His alcoholic problem was so complex, and his depression so great, that we felt his only hope would be through what we then called "moral psychology," and we doubted if even that would have any effect. However, he did adopt the ideas contained in this book. He has not had a drink for more than three years. I see him now and then, and he is as fine a specimen of manhood as one could wish to meet.[20]

VIII. WILLIAM GRIFFITH WILSON

BASIC CONCEPTS OF
ALCOHOLICS ANONYMOUS
William Griffith Wilson 1944

Alcoholics Anonymous is an informal fellowship of about 12,000 formerly alcoholic men and women who are to be found banded together as groups in about three hundred and twenty-five American and Canadian communities, these groups ranging in size from half a dozen to many hundreds of individuals. Our oldest members have been sober eight to nearly ten years. Of those sincerely willing to stop drinking, about 50 percent have done so at once, 25 percent after a few relapses, and most of the remainder have improved. It is probable that half of our members, had they not been drinkers, would have appeared in ordinary life to be normal people. The other half would have appeared as more or less pronounced neurotic.

Alcoholics Anonymous, or "AA," popularly so-called, has but one purpose—one objective only—"To help other alcoholics to recover from their illness."

Nothing is asked of the alcoholic approaching us save a desire on his part to get well. He subscribes to no membership requirements, no fees or dues, nor is a belief in any particular point of view, medical or religious, demanded of him. As a group we take no position on any controversial question. Emphatically, we are not evangelists or reformers. Being alcoholics who have recovered, we aim to help only those who want to get well. We do this because we have found that working with other alcoholics plays such a vital part in keeping us all sober.

You may inquire, "Just how does AA work?" I cannot

fully answer that question. Many AA techniques have been adopted after a ten-year process of trial and error which has led to some interesting results. But, as laymen, we doubt our own ability to explain them. We can only tell you what we do, and what seems, from our point of view, to happen to us.

At the very outset we should like it made ever so clear that AA is a synthetic concept—a synthetic gadget, as it were, drawing upon the resources of medicine, psychiatry, religion, and our own experience of drinking and recovery. You will search in vain for a single new fundamental. We have merely streamlined old and proved principles of psychiatry and religion into such forms that the alcoholic will accept them. And then we have created a society of his own kind where he can enthusiastically put these very principles to work on himself and other sufferers.

Then, too, we have tried hard to capitalize our one great natural advantage. That advantage is, of course, our personal experience as drinkers who have recovered. How often the doctors and clergymen throw up their hands when, after exhaustive treatment or exhortation, the alcoholic still insists, "But you don't understand me. You never did any serious drinking yourself, so how can you? Neither can you show me many who have recovered."

Now, when one alcoholic who has got well talks to another who hasn't, such objections seldom arise, for the new man sees in a few minutes that he is talking to a kindred spirit, one who understands. Neither can the recovered AA member be deceived, for he knows every trick, every rationalization of the drinking game. So the usual barriers go down with a crash. Mutual confidence, that indispensable of all therapy, follows as surely as day does night. And if this absolutely necessary rapport is not forthcoming at once it is almost certain to develop when the new man has met other AAs. Someone will, as we say, "click with him."

As soon as that happens we have a good chance of selling our prospect those very essentials which you doctors have so long advocated, and the problem drinker finds our society a congenial place to work them out for himself and his fellow alcoholic. For the first time in years he thinks himself understood and he feels useful; uniquely useful, indeed, as he takes his own turn promoting the recovery of others. No matter what the outer world still thinks of him, he now knows that he can get well, for he stands in the midst of scores of cases worse than his own who have attained the goal. And there are other cases precisely like his own—a pressure of testimony which usually overwhelms him. If he doesn't succumb at once, he will almost surely do so later when Barleycorn builds a still hotter fire under him, thus blocking off all his other carefully planned exits from dilemma. The speaker recalls seventy-five failures during the first three years of AA—people we utterly gave up. During the past seven years sixty-two of these people have returned to us, most of them now making good. They tell us they returned because they knew they would die or go mad if they didn't. Having tried everything else within their means and having exhausted their pet rationalizations, they came back and took their medicine. That is why we never need to evangelize alcoholics. If still in their right minds they come back, once they have been well exposed to AA.

Now to recapitulate. Alcoholics Anonymous has made two major contributions to the program of psychiatry and religion. These are, it seems to us, the long-missing links in the chain of recovery:

1.   Our ability, as ex-drinkers, to secure the confidence of the new man—to "build a transmission line into him."

2.   The provision of an understanding society of ex-drinkers in which the newcomer can successfully apply the principles of medicine and religion to himself and others.

So far as we AAs are concerned, these principles, now used by us every day, seem to be in surprising agreement.   Let's compare briefly what in a general way medicine and religion tell the alcoholic:

Medicine Says

1. The alcoholic needs a personality change.
2. The patient ought to be analyzed and should make a full and honest mental catharsis.
3. Serious personality defects must be cured through accurate self-knowledge and realistic readjustment to life.
4. The alcoholic neurotic retreats from life, is a picture of anxiety and abnormal self concern; he withdraws from the "herd."
5. The alcoholic must find "a new compelling interest in life," must "get back into the herd."   He should find an interesting occupation, should join clubs, social activities, political parties, or discover hobbies to take the place of alcohol.

Religion Says

1. The alcoholic needs a change of heart, a spiritual awakening.
2. The alcoholic should make examination of the "conscience" and a confession—or a moral inventory and a frank discussion.
3. Character defects (sins) can be eliminated by acquiring more honesty, humility, unselfishness, tolerance, generosity, love, etc.
4. The alcoholic's basic trouble is self-centeredness. Filled with fear and self-seeking, he has forgotten the brotherhood of man.
5. The alcoholic should learn the "expulsive power of a new affection," love of serving man, of serving God. He must "lose his life to find it"; he should join the church and there find self-forgetfulness in service.   For "faith without works is dead."

Thus far, religion and medicine are seen in hearty accord. But in one respect they do differ. When the doctor has shown the alcoholic his underlying difficulties and has prescribed a program of readjustment, he says to him, "Now that you understand what is required for recovery, you should no longer depend on me. You must depend upon yourself. *You go do it.*"

Clearly, then, the object of the doctor is to make the patient self-sufficient and largely, if not wholly, dependent upon himself.

Religion does not attempt this. It says that *faith in self is not enough*, even for a nonalcoholic. The clergyman says that we shall have to find and depend upon a higher power—God. He advises prayer and frankly recommends an attitude of unwavering reliance upon Him who presides over all. By this means we discover a strength much beyond our own resources.

So, the main difference seems to add up to this. Medicine says, "Know yourself, be strong, and you will be able to face life." Religion says, "Know thyself, ask God for power, and you become truly free."

In Alcoholics Anonymous the new man may try either method. He sometimes eliminates "the spiritual angle" from Twelve Steps to Recovery and wholly relies upon honesty, tolerance, and "working with others." But it is curious and interesting to note that faith always comes to those who try this simple approach *with an open mind*—and in the meantime they stay sober.

If, however, the spiritual content of the Twelve Steps is actively denied, they can seldom remain dry. That is our AA experience everywhere. We stress the spiritual simply because thousands of us have found we can't do without it.

At this point I should like to state the Twelve Steps of the Alcoholics Anonymous Program of Recovery so that you physicians may accurately compare your methods with ours.

The Twelve Steps

1. We admitted we were powerless over alcohol—that our lives had become unmanageable.
2. Came to believe that a Power greater than ourselves could restore us to sanity.
3. Made a decision to turn our will and our lives over to the care of God *as we understood Him.*
4. Made a searching and fearless moral inventory of ourselves.
5. Admitted to God, to ourselves, and to another human being the exact nature of our wrongs.
6. Were entirely ready to have God remove all these defects of character.
7. Humbly asked Him to remove our shortcomings.
8. Made a list of all persons we had harmed, and became willing to make amends to them all.
9. Made direct amends to such people wherever possible, except when to do so would injure them or others.
10. Continued to take personal inventory and when we were wrong promptly admitted it.
11. Sought, through prayer and meditation, to improve our conscious contact with God *as we understood Him*, praying only for knowledge of His will for us and the power to carry that out.
12. Having had a spiritual awakening as the result of these steps, we tried to carry this message to alcoholics, and to practice these principles in all our affairs.

Boiled down, these steps mean, simply: (1) admission of alcoholism; (2) personality analysis and catharsis; (3) adjustment of personal relations; (4) dependence upon some higher power; and (5) working with other alcoholics.

Most strongly, we point out that adherence to these principles is not a condition of AA membership. Any alcoholic who admits he has a problem is an AA member regardless of how much he disagrees with the program. Based upon our experience, the whole program is a suggestion only. The alcoholic, objecting at first to the spiritual factor, is urged to keep an open mind, meanwhile treating his own AA group as "a power greater than himself." Under these conditions the newcomer commences to undergo a personality change at such a rate and of such dimensions that he cannot fully account for it on the basis of self-realization and self-discipline. Not only does his alcoholic obsession disappear, but he finds himself progressively free of fear, resentment, and inferiority. These changes seem to have come about almost automatically. Hence he concludes that "a power greater than himself" must indeed have been at work. Having come to this point, he begins to form his own concept of God. He then develops confidence in that concept, which grows as he gets proof in everyday life that his new faith actually works, really produces results.

This is what most AAs are trying to say when they talk about a spiritual experience. They mean a certain quality of personality change which, in their belief, could not have occurred without the help and presence of the creative spirit of the universe.

With the average AA, many months may elapse before he is aware of faith in the spiritual sense. Yet I know scarcely an

AA member of more than a year's standing who still thinks his transformation was a wholly psychologic phenomenon based entirely upon his own normal resources. Almost every one of our members will tell you that, while he may not go along with a clergyman's concept of God, he has developed one of his own on which he can positively depend—one which works for him.

We AAs are quite indifferent to what people may call this spiritual experience of ours. But to us it looks very much like conversion, the very thing most alcoholics have sworn they never would have. In fact, I am beginning to believe that we shall have to call it just that, for I know our good friend, Dr. Harry Tiebout, is sitting here in this room. As you may know, he is the psychiatrist who recently told his own professional Society, The American Psychiatric Association, that what we AAs get is conversion—sure enough and no fooling! And if the spirit of that great psychologist, William James, could be consulted, he'd doubtless refer us to his famous book, *Varieties of Religious Experience*, in which personality change through the "educational variety of spiritual experience, or conversion" is so ably explored. Whatever this mysterious process is, it certainly seems to work, and with us who are on the way to the asylum or the undertaker, anything that works looks very, very good indeed.

And I'm very happy to say that many other distinguished members of your profession have pronounced our Twelve Steps good medicine. Clergymen of all denominations say they are good religion, and of course we AAs like them because they do work. Most ardently we hope that every physician here today will find himself able to share this happy agreement. In the early years of AA, it seemed to us alcoholics that we wandered in a sort of no-man's-land which appeared to divide science and religion. But all that has changed since AA has now become a common meeting ground for both concepts.

Yes, Alcoholics Anonymous is a cooperative venture. All cases requiring physical treatment are referred to you physicians. We frequently work with the psychiatrist and often find that he can do and say things to a patient which we cannot. He, in turn, avails himself of the fact that as ex-alcoholics we can sometimes walk in where he fears to tread. Throughout the country we are in daily touch with hospitals and sanitariums, both public and private. The enthusiastic support given us by so many of your noted institutions is something for which we are deeply grateful. The opportunity to work with alcoholics means everything; to most of us it means life itself. Without the chance to forget our own troubles by helping others out of theirs, we would certainly perish. That is the heart of AA—it is our lifeblood.

We have torn still other pages from the Book of Medicine, putting them to practical use. It is from you gentlemen we learn that alcoholism is a complex malady; that abnormal drinking is but a symptom of personal maladjustment to life; that, as a class, we alcoholics are apt to be sensitive, emotionally immature, grandiose in our demands upon ourselves and others; that we have usually "gone broke" on some dream ideal of perfection; that, failing to realize the dream, we sensitive folk escape cold reality by taking to the bottle; that this habit of escape finally turns into an obsession, or, as you gentlemen put it, a compulsion to drink so subtly powerful that no disaster, however great, even near death or insanity, can, in most cases, seem to break it; that we are the victims of the age-old alcoholic dilemma: our obsession guarantees that we shall go on drinking, but our increasing physical sensitivity guarantees that we shall go insane or die if we do.

When these facts, coming from the mouths of you gentlemen of science, are poured by an AA member into the person of another alcoholic they strike deep—the effect is shattering. That inflated ego, those elaborate rationalizations by which our neurotic friend has been trying to erect self-sufficiency on a foundation of inferiority, begin to ooze out of him. Sometimes his deflation is like the collapse of a toy balloon at the approach of a hot poker. But deflation is just what we AAs are looking for. It is our universal experience that unless we can start deflation, and so self-realization, we get nowhere at all. The more utterly we can smash the delusion that the alcoholic can get over alcoholism "on his own," or that someday he may be able to drink like a gentleman, the more successful we are bound to be.

In fact, we aim to produce a crisis, to cause him to "hit bottom," as AAs say. Of course you will understand that this is all done by indirection. We never pronounce sentences, nor do we tell any alcoholic what he *must* do. We don't even tell him he is an alcoholic. Relating the seriousness of our own cases, we leave him to draw his own conclusions. But once he has accepted the fact that he is and the further fact that he is powerless to recover unaided, the battle is half won. As the AAs have it, "he is hooked." He is caught as if in a psychologic vise.

If the jaws of it do not grip him tightly enough at first, more drinking will almost invariably turn up the screw to the point where he will cry "Enough!" Then, as we say, he is "softened up." This reduces him to a state of complete dependence on whatever or whoever can stop his drinking. He is in exactly the same mental fix as the cancer patient who becomes dependent, abjectly dependent, if you will, on what you men of science can do for cancer. Better still, he becomes "sweetly reasonable," truly open-minded, as only the dying can do.

Under these conditions, accepting the spiritual implications of the AA program presents no difficulty even to the sophisticate. About half the AA members were once agnostics or atheists. This dispels the notion that we are only effective with the religiously susceptible. You remember the now famous remark, "There are no atheists in the foxholes." So it is with most alcoholics. Bring them within range of the AA and "blockbusters" will soon land near enough to start radical changes in outlook, attitude, and personality.

These are some of the basic factors which perhaps partly account for such success as we have had. I wish time permitted me to give you an intimate glimpse of our life together, of our meetings, of our social side, of those fast friendships unlike any we had known before, of our participation by thousands in the war effort and the armed services, where so many AAs are discovering that they can face up to reality—no longer institutionalized, even within an AA Group. We have all found that God can be relied upon both in Alaska and India, that strength can come out of weakness, that perhaps only those who have tasted the fruits of reliance upon a higher power can fully understand the true meaning of personal liberty, freedom of the human spirit.

Surely, you who are here this morning must realize how much we AAs are beholden to you, how much we have borrowed from you, how much we still depend upon you. For you have supplied us ammunition which we have used as your lay assistants—gun pointers for your artillery. I have put out for inspection our version of the factors which bring about personality change, our method of analysis, catharsis, and adjustment.

I have tried to show you a little of our great new compelling interest in life—this society where men and women understand each other, where the clamors of self are lost in our great common objective, where we can learn enough of patience, tolerance, honesty, humility, and service to subdue our former masters—insecurity, resentment, and unsatisfied dreams of power.

But I must not close without paying tribute to our partner, Religion. Like Medicine, it is indispensable. At this temple of science I hope none will take it amiss if I give Religion the last word:

"God grant us the serenity to accept the things we cannot change, courage to change the things we can, and wisdom to know the difference."[21]

IX. HARRY TIEBOUT, M.D.

THE EGO FACTORS IN
SURRENDER IN ALCOHOLISM
Harry Tiebout, M.D. 1954

In the past 15 years, my understanding of the nature of alcoholism as a disease has been influenced largely by insight into the mechanisms at work in the Alcoholics Anonymous process. Some years ago I stated that AA, to succeed, must induce a surrender on the part of the individual.[1] More recently, I discussed the idea of compliance[2] acting as a barrier to that real acceptance which a surrender produces. On this occasion I propose to extend my observations by discussing (a) what factors in the individual must surrender, and (b) how the surrender reaction changes the inner psychic picture.

The first question, what factors in the individual must surrender, received passing attention in the article on compliance. There, relative to the difficulty of surrender, I noted that "the presence of an apparently unconquerable ego became evident. It was this ego which had to become humble." The first part of the present communication will be devoted to an elaboration of the nature of this ego factor.

Use of the word "ego" involves always the possibility of confusion of meaning. For a time, therefore, I considered a substitute term. That idea was set aside because, despite possible misinterpretation, the word ego is current in everyday language in exactly the sense in which it will be employed in this discussion. The expression, "he has an inflated ego," is self-explanatory. It evokes the picture of a pompous, self-important, strutting individual whose inferiorities are masked by a surface assurance. Such a person appears thick-skinned, insensitive, nearly impervious to the existence of others, a completely self-centered individual who plows unthinkingly through life, intent on gathering unto himself all the comforts and satisfactions available. He is generally considered the epitome of selfishness, and there the matter rests.

This popular view of ego, while it may not have scientific foundation, has one decided value: it possesses a meaning and can convey a concept which the average person can grasp. This concept of the inflated ego recognizes the common ancestor of a whole series of traits, namely, that they are all manifestations of an underlying feeling state in which personal considerations are first and foremost.

The existence of this ego has long been recognized, but a difficulty in terminology still remains. Part of the difficulty arises from the use of the word ego, in psychiatric and psychological circles, to designate those elements of the psyche which are supposed to rule psychic life. Freud divided mental life into three major subdivisions: the id, the ego, and the superego. The first, he stated, contains the feeling of life on a deep, instinctual level; the third is occupied by the conscience, whose function is to put brakes on the impulses arising within the id. The ego should act as mediator between the demands of the id and the restraints of the superego, which might be over-zealous and bigoted. Freud's own research was concerned mainly with the activities of the id and the superego. The void he left with respect to the ego is one that his followers are endeavoring to fill, but as yet with no generally accepted conclusions.

Ego: By Two Definitions

The word ego, however, has been preempted by the psychiatrists and psychologists, although they do not always agree among themselves about the meaning to be attached to it. The resulting confusion is the more lamentable because almost everyone, layman or scientist, would agree on the concept of the inflated ego. It would be helpful if other terms were found for the ego concepts about which there are differing views.

The solution for this dilemma will be to indicate with a capital E the big Ego, and without a capital to identify the personality aspect which Freud had in mind when he placed ego between id and superego.[3]

With this disposition of the problem of terminology, it is now possible to consider the first issue, namely, the Ego factors in the alcoholic which, through surrender, become humble. The concept of the enlarged Ego, as noted previously, is available to common observation. Those who do not recognize it in themselves can always see it in some member of their family or among friends and acquaintances—not to mention patients. Everyone knows egotistical people and has a perfectly clear idea of what the word means. Besides egotistical, and the series of words mentioned earlier, adjectives which help to round out the portrait of the egotistical person are prideful, arrogant, pushing, dominating, attention-seeking, aggressive, opinionated, headstrong, stubborn, determined, and impatient.

All these terms are inadequate, however, because they describe only surface features without conveying any feeling of the inner essence from which the Ego springs. Unless some appreciation for the source of the Ego is gained, the dynamic import is lost and the term may seem merely a form of name-calling. It is easy to say someone has a big Ego without awareness of what is really happening in the deep layers of that person's mind, without perception of the Ego. Nor is it a matter of intellect. The need here is to lay hold of the inner feeling elements upon which the activity of the Ego rests. Only when these elements become clear can the fundamental basis of the Ego also be clarified.

It is convenient, for the exposition of this inner functioning, to reverse the usual sequence and to present a conclusion in advance of the evidence on which it is based. This is, briefly, that the Ego is made up of the persisting elements, in the adult psyche, of the original nature of the child.

Certain aspects of the infant's psyche may be usefully examined. There are three factors which should receive mention. The first is, as Freud observed in his priceless phrase "His Majesty the Baby," that the infant is born ruler of all he surveys. He comes from the Nirvana of the womb, where he is usually the sole occupant, and he clings to that omnipotence with an innocence, yet determination, which baffles parent after parent. The second, stemming directly from the monarch within, is that the infant tolerates frustration poorly and lets the world know it readily. The third significant aspect of the child's original psyche is its tendency to do everything in a hurry. Observe youngsters on the beach: they run rather than walk. Observe them coming on a visit: the younger ones tear from the car while their elder siblings adopt a more leisurely pace. The three-year-olds, and more so the twos, cannot engage in play requiring long periods of concentration. Whatever they are doing must be done quickly. As the same children age, they gradually become able to stick to one activity for longer times.

Thus at the start of life the psyche (1) assumes its own omnipotence, (2) cannot accept frustrations and (3) functions at a tempo allegretto with a good deal of staccato and vivace thrown in.

Now the question is, "If the infantile psyche persists into adult life, how will its presence be manifested?"

In general, when infantile traits continue into adulthood, the person is spoken of as immature, a label often applied with little comprehension of the reason for its accuracy. It is necessary to link these three traits from the original psyche with immaturity and, at the same time, show how they affect the adult psyche. If this is done, not only will the correctness of the appellation "immature" be apparent but, moreover, a feeling for the nature of the unconscious underpinnings of the Ego will have been created.

Recognizing Immaturity

Two steps can aid in recognizing the relationship between immaturity and a continuance of the infantile elements. The first is, by an act of imagination, to set these original traits into an adult unconscious. The validity of this procedure is founded upon modern knowledge of the nature of the forces operating in the unconscious of people of mature age. The second step is to estimate the effect that the prolongation of these infantile qualities will have upon the adult individual.

This attempt should not strain the imagination severely. Take, for instance, the third of the qualities common to the original psychic state, namely, the tendency to act hurriedly. If that tendency prevails in the unconscious, what must the result be? The individual will certainly do everything in a hurry. He will think fast, talk fast, and live fast, or he will spend an inordinate amount of time and energy holding his fast-driving proclivities in check.

Often the net result will be an oscillation between periods of speeding ahead followed by periods during which the direction of the force is reversed, the brakes (superego) being applied in equally vigorous fashion. The parallel of this in the behavior of the alcoholic will not be lost on those who have had experience with this class of patients.

Let us take the same trait of doing everything in a hurry and apply it to the word "immature." Few will deny that jumping at conclusions, doing things as speedily as possible, give evidence of immaturity. It is youth that drives fast, thinks fast, feels fast, moves fast, acts hastily in most situations. There can be little question that one of the hallmarks of the immature is the proneness to be under inner pressure for accomplishment. Big plans, big schemes, big hopes abound, unfortunately not matched by an ability to produce. But the effect upon the adult of the persisting infantile quality to do everything in less than sufficient time can now be seen in a clearer light. The adult trait is surely a survival from the original psyche of the infant.

The two other surviving qualities of the infantile psyche similarly contribute to the picture of immaturity and also, indirectly, help to clarify the nature of the Ego with a capital E. The first of these, the feeling of omnipotence, when carried over into adult life, affects the individual in ways easily anticipated. Omnipotence is, of course, associated with royalty, if not divinity. The unconscious result of the persistence of this trait is that its bearer harbors a belief of his own special role and in his own exceptional rights. Such a person finds it well-nigh impossible to function happily on an ordinary level. Obsessed with divine afflatus, the thought of operating in the lowly and humble areas of life is most distressing to him. The very idea that such a place is all one is capable of occupying is in itself a blow to the Ego, which reacts with a sense of inferiority at its failure to fill a more distinguished position. Moreover, any success becomes merely Ego fodder, boosting the individual's rating of himself to increasingly unrealistic proportions as the king side eagerly drinks in this evidence of special worth.

The ability to administer the affairs of state, both large and small, is taken for granted. The belief that he is a natural executive placed in the wrong job merely confirms his conviction that, at best, he is the victim of lack of appreciation, and at worst, of sabotage by jealous people who set up roadblocks to his progress. The world is inhabited by selfish people, intent only on their own advancement.

The genesis of all this is beyond his perception. To tell him that his reactions spring from the demands of an inner unsatisfied king is to invite incredulity and disbelief, so far from the conscious mind are any such thoughts or feelings. People who openly continue to cling to their claims of divine prerogative usually end up in a world especially constructed for their care. In others, the omnipotence pressures are rather better buried. The individual may admit that, in many ways, he acts like a spoiled brat, but he is scarcely conscious of the extent of the tendency, nor how deeply rooted it may be. He, like most people, resolutely avoids a careful look because the recognition of any such inner attitudes is highly disturbing. The unconscious credence in one's special prerogatives savors too much of straight selfishness to be anything but unpleasant to contemplate.

And so, for the most part, people remain happily ignorant of the unconscious drives which push them around. They may wonder why they tend to boil inside and wish they could free themselves from a constant sense of uneasiness and unsettlement. They may recognize that they seem jittery and easily excited and long for the time when they can meet life more calmly and maturely; they may hate their tendency to become rattled. But their insight into the origin of all this is next to nothing, if not a complete blank. The king lies deep below the surface, far out of sight.

Inability to Accept Frustration

The last trait carried over from infancy is the inability to accept frustration. In an obvious sense, this inability is another aspect of the king within, since one of the prerogatives of royalty is to proceed without interruption. For the king to wait is an affront to the royal rank, a slap in at his majesty. The ramifications of this inability to endure frustration are widespread, and the significance of much that occurs in the behavior of the alcoholic is so far-reaching, that it seems advisable to discuss this trait under a separate heading.

As already indicated, on the surface the inability of the king to accept frustration is absolutely logical. The wish of the king is the law of the land, and especially in the land of infancy. Any frustration is clearly a direct threat to the status of his majesty, whose whole being is challenged by the untoward interruption.

Even more significant is another aspect of this inner imperiousness. Behind it lies the assumption that the individual should not be stopped. Again, this is logical if one considers how an absolute monarch operates. He simply does not expect to be stopped; as he wills, so will he do. This trait, persisting in the unconscious, furnishes a constant pressure driving the individual forward. It says, in essence, "I am unstoppable!"

The unconscious which cannot be stopped views life entirely from the angle of whether or not a stopping is likely, imminent, or not at all in the picture. When a stopping is likely, there is worry and perhaps depression. When it seems imminent, there is anxiety bordering on panic, and when the threat is removed, there is relief and gaiety. Health is equated with a feeling of buoyancy and smooth sailing ahead, a sense of "I feel wonderful!" Sickness, contrariwise, means lacking vim, vigor, and vitality, and is burdened with a sense of "I'm not getting anywhere." The need to "get somewhere" to "be on the go," and the consequent suffering from eternal restlessness, is still another direct effect of an inner inability to be stopped or, expressed otherwise, to accept the fact that one is limited. The king not only cannot accept the normal frustrations of life but, because of his inordinate driving ahead, is constantly creating unnecessary roadblocks by virtue of his own insistence on barging ahead, thus causing added trouble for himself.

Of course, on some occasions, the king gets stopped, and stopped totally. Illness, arrest, sometimes the rules and regulations of life, will halt him. Then he marks time, complies if need be, waiting for the return of freedom, which he celebrates in the time-honored fashion if he is an alcoholic: he gets drunk, initiating a phase when there is no stopping him.

The immaturity of such a person is readily evident. He is impatient of delay, can never let matters evolve; he must have a blueprint to follow, outlining clearly a path through the jungle of life. The wisdom of the ages is merely shackling tradition which should make way for the freshness, the insouciance of youth. The value of staying where one is, and working out one's destiny in the here and now, is not suspected. The 24-hour principle would be confining for one whose inner life brooks no confinement. The unstoppable person seeks life, fun, adventure, excitement, and discovers he is on a perpetual whirligig which carries him continuously ahead—but, of course, in a circle. The unstoppable person has not time for growth. He must always, inwardly, feel immature.

This, then, is how the carry-over of infantile traits affects the adult so encumbered. He is possessed by an inner king who not only must do things in a hurry, but has no capacity for taking frustration in stride. He seeks a life which will not stop him and finds himself in a ceaseless rat race.

All this is part and parcel of the big Ego. The individual has no choice. He cannot select one characteristic and hang on to that, shedding other more obviously undesirable traits. It is all or nothing. For example, the driving person usually has plenty of energy, spark, vivacity. He stands out as a most attractive human being. Clinging to that quality, however, merely insures the continuance of excessive drive and Ego, with all the pains attendant upon a life based on those qualities. The sacrifice of the Ego elements must be total, or they will soon regain their ascendancy.

Learning To Live

Those who view the prospect of life without abundant drive as inutterably dull and boring should examine the life of members of Alcoholics Anonymous who have truly adopted the

AA program. They will see people who have been stopped—
and who, therefore, do not have to go anywhere—but people
who are learning, for the first time in their lives, to live. They
are neither dull nor wishy-washy. Quite the contrary, they are
alive and interested in the realities about them. They see things
in the large, are tolerant, open-minded, not close-minded bull-
ing ahead. They are receptive to the wonders in the world about
them, including the presence of a Deity who makes all this
possible. They are the ones who are really living. The attainment of such a way of life is no mean accomplishment.

Preliminary to this discussion, the conclusion was offered
that the Ego was a residual of the initial feeling life of the infant.
It should be evident that the immaturity characteristically found
in the make-up of the alcoholic is a persistence of the original
state of the child. In connection with the description of the
manifestations which denote a large and active Ego, it should be
recalled that the presence in the unconscious of such Ego forces
may be quite out of reach of the conscious observation. Only
through the acting and feeling of the individual can their
existence be suspected.

Now the answer to the first question raised herein, namely,
what part of the alcoholic must surrender, is obvious: it is the
Ego element.

Life without Ego is no new conception. Two thousand
years ago, Christ preached the necessity of losing one's life in
order to find it again. He did not say Ego, but that was what he
had in mind. The analysts of our time recognize the same truth;
they talk also about ego reduction. Freud saw therapy as a
running battle between the original narcissism of the infant (his
term for Ego) and the therapist whose task it was to reduce that

original state to more manageable proportions. Since Freud could not conceive of life without some measure of Ego, he never resolved the riddle of how contentment is achieved; for him, man to the end was doomed to strife and unhappiness, his dearest desires sure to be frustrated by an unfriendly world.

In his studies on the addictions, Rado[3] more explicitly asserts that the Ego must be reduced. He first portrays the Ego as follows: "Once it was a baby, radiant with self-esteem, full of belief in the omnipotence of its wishes, of its thoughts, gestures and words." Then, on the process of Ego-reduction: "But the child's megalomania melted away under the inexorable pressure of experience. Its sense of its own sovereignty had to make room for a more modest self-evaluation. This process, first described by Freud, may be designated the reduction in size of the original ego; it is a painful procedure and one that is possibly never completely carried out."

No Compromise With Ego

Like Freud, Rado thinks only in terms of reduction; the need for the complete elimination of Ego is a stand which they cannot bring themselves to assume. Hence they unwittingly advocate the retention of some infantile traits, with no clear awareness that trading with the devil, the Ego, no matter how carefully safeguarded, merely keeps him alive and likely at any occasion to erupt full force into action. There can be no successful compromise with Ego, a fact not sufficiently appreciated by many, if not most, therapists.

Thus the dilemma encountered in ego-reduction would be best resolved by recognizing that the old Ego must go and a new one take its place. Then no issue would arise about how much of the earliest elements may be retained. The answer, theoretically, is none. Actually the total banishment of the initial state is difficult to achieve. Man can only grow in the direction of its complete elimination. Its final expulsion is a goal which can only be hoped for.

The second question raised here is, "How does the surrender reaction change the inner psychic picture?" This question is based on a presupposition, namely that surrender is an emotional step in which the Ego, at least for the time being, acknowledges that it is no longer supreme. This acknowledgment is valueless if limited to consciousness; it must be accompanied by similar feelings in the unconscious. For the alcoholic, surrender is marked by the admission of being powerless over alcohol. His sobriety has that quality of peace and tranquility which makes for a lasting quiet within only if the surrender is effective in the unconscious and permanent as well.

The effects of surrender upon the psyche are extremely logical: The traits listed as characteristic of the Ego influence are canceled out. The opposite of king is the commoner. Appropriately, Alcoholics Anonymous stresses humility. The opposite of impatience is the ability to take things in stride, to make an inner reality of the slogan, "Easy does it." The opposite of drive is staying in one position, where one can be open-minded, receptive, and responsive.

This picture of the non-Ego type of person might be amplified in many directions but to do so would serve no immediate purpose. To have discussed the effect of the Ego upon behavior, and to have pointed out what may happen when the Ego is at least temporarily knocked out of action, is sufficient to make the point of this communication: It is the Ego which is the arch-enemy of sobriety, and it is the Ego which must be disposed of if the individual is to attain a new way of life.

Up to this point, no clinical material has been submitted to confirm the ideas presented. Their validity will be apparent to many therapists. One brief citation from clinical experience will be offered, however, in the hope that it may serve as a concrete illustration of these ideas.

The patient, a man in his late 30s, had a long history of alcoholism, with 7 years of futile attempts to recover through Alcoholics Anonymous, interspersed with countless admissions to "drying out" places. Then, for reasons not completely clear, he decided to take a drastic step. He determined to enter a sanitarium and place himself in the hands of a psychiatrist, a hitherto unheard of venture. He telephoned to arrange for a limited stay at a sanitarium where he could have regular interviews with me.

From the outset, he was undeniably in earnest, although it was only after the first interview that he really let go and could talk freely about himself and the things that were going on inside him. After the usual preliminaries, the first interview started with a discussion of feelings and how they operate. The patient was questioned about the word Ego as used at AA meetings. He confessed his ignorance of its true meaning and listened with interest to brief remarks on how it works. Before long, he was locating in himself some of the Ego forces which hitherto he had been vigorously denying because they savored too much of vanity and selfishness. With that recognition, the patient made a revealing remark. He said, in all sincerity, "My goodness, I never knew that. You don't do your thinking up here (pointing to his head), you think down here where you feel" (placing his hands on his stomach). He was learning that his feelings has a "mind" of their own and that unless he heeded what they were saying, he could easily get into trouble. He was facing the actuality of his Ego as a feeling element in his life, a step he was able to take because he was no longer going at full steam ahead. His decision to place himself under care, a surrender of a sort, had quieted him and made him receptive, able to observe what was going on in himself. It was the beginning of a real inventory.

The next insight he uncovered was even more startling. He had been requested routinely to report any dreams he would have. Much to his surprise, they appeared regularly during the period of contact. In his fifth dream, the patient found himself locked up in an institution because of his drinking. The interpretation offered, based upon relevant materials, was that the patient equated any kind of stopping with being locked up; that his real difficulty lay in the fact that he could not tolerate being stopped, and abstaining was merely another stopping he could not take. The patient's reaction to the interpretation was most significant. He remained silent for some little time; then he began to talk, saying, "I tell you, Doc, it was like this. I'd get drunk, maybe stay on it 2 or 3 days, then I'd go into one of those drying out places where I'd stay 5 or 6 days and I'd be all over wanting a drink. Then I'd come out and stay sober, maybe a week, maybe a month, but pretty soon the thought would come into my mind, I want to drink! Maybe I'd go and I'd order a drink, but I wouldn't drink it right off. I'd put it on the bar and I'd look at it and I'd think and then I'd look and think: King for a day!" The connection between Ego and his own conduct had become explicit, as well as the relationship between not being stopped and Ego. He saw clearly that when he took that drink, he was the boss once more. Any previous reduction of Ego had been only temporary.

In treatment, the problem is to make that reduction of Ego permanent. Therapy is centered on the ways and means, first, of bringing the Ego to earth, and second, keeping it there. The discussion of this methodology would be out of place here, but it is relevant to emphasize one point, namely the astonishing capacity of the Ego to pass out of the picture and then reenter it, blithe and intact. A patient's dream neatly depicted this quality. This patient dreamt that he was on the twelfth-floor balcony of a New York hotel. He threw a rubber ball to the pavement below and saw it rebound to the level of the balcony. Much to his amazement, the ball again dropped and again rebounded to the same height. This continued for an indefinite period and, as he was watching, a clock in a neighboring church spire struck nine. Like the cat with nine lives, the Ego has a marvelous capacity to scramble back to safety—a little ruffled, perhaps, but soon operating with all its former aplomb, convinced once more that now it, the Ego, can master all events and push on ahead.

The capacity of the Ego to bypass experience is astounding and would be humorous were it not so tragic in its consequences. Cutting the individual down to size and making the results last is a task never completely accomplished. The possibility of a return of his Ego must be faced by every alcoholic. If it does return, he may refrain from drinking, but he will surely go on a "dry drunk," with all the old feelings and attitudes once more asserting themselves and making sobriety a shambles of discontent and restlessness. Not until the ego is decisively retired can peace and quiet again prevail. As one sees this struggle in process, the need for the helping hand of a Deity becomes clearer. Mere man alone all too often seems powerless to stay the force of his Ego. He needs assistance and needs it urgently.

Summary

In the process of surrender which the alcoholic necessarily undergoes before his alcoholism can be arrested, the part of the personality which must surrender is the inflated Ego. This aspect of personality was identified as immature traits carried over from infancy into adulthood, specifically, a feeling of omnipotence, inability to tolerate frustration, and excessive drive, exhibited in the need to do all things precipitously. The manner in which surrender affects the Ego was discussed and illustrated briefly from clinical experience. The object of therapy is to permanently replace the old Ego and its activity.[22]

References

[1]Tiebout, H.M. "The Act of Surrender in the Therapeutic Process." With special reference to alcoholism. Quart. J. Stud. Alc. 10: 48-58, 1949.

[2]Tiebout, H.M. "Surrender Versus Compliance in Therapy." With special reference to alcoholism. Quart. J. Stud. Alc. 14: 58-68, 1953.

[3]Rado, S. "The Psychoanalysis of Pharmachothymia (drug addiction). The clinical picture." Psychoanal. Quart. 2: 1-23, 1933.

X. RICHMOND WALKER

SURRENDERING YOUR LIFE

It seems to me the basic fact of the AA program is some faith in a Higher Power. Over a period of drinking years, we've proved to ourselves and to everybody else that we can't stop drinking by our own willpower. We have been proved helpless before the power of alcohol. So the only way we could stop drinking was by turning to a Power greater than ourselves. I call that power God. The time when a person really gets this program, I think, is when they get down on their knees and surrender themselves to God, as they understand Him.

Surrender means putting your life into God's hands and making a promise to Him that you will try to live the way He wants you to live. After you've made this surrender, the drink problem is out of your hands and in the hands of God. The thing you have to do is to be sure that you never reach out and take the problem back into your own hands. Leave it in God's hands. Whenever you're tempted to take a drink, just say to yourself: I can't do that. I've made a bargain with God not to drink. I know God doesn't want me to drink so I won't do it. And at the same time, say a little prayer to God for the strength you need to keep your bargain with Him.

Having surrendered your life to God and put your drink problem in His hands doesn't mean that you'll never be tempted to drink. So you must build up strength for the time when temptation will come. I have a little quiet time every morning before breakfast. I read a little, write a little, and pray a little. I get my mind in the right mood for the day. Starting the day right is a great help in keeping sober. As the days go by you get used to a sober life; it gets easier and easier. You begin to develop a deep gratitude to God for saving you from that terrible life of drawing blanks and fighting hangovers. And you begin to enjoy peace and serenity and real, quiet happiness. As long as you live the way God wants you to live, you're all right.[23]

READING THE BOOK—
SEVEN THINGS TO DO

When I read the book *Alcoholics Anonymous*, I found out what I had to do to get away from alcohol. I had to do seven things.

First, I had to admit that I was definitely an alcoholic. That wasn't easy because I had to swallow my pride and admit that I was different from ordinary drinkers. Of course, my wife knew it long before I did, but finally I had to admit it even to her.

Second, I had to accept the fact that I must spend the rest of my life without liquor. At first, I found it hard to visualize life without ever taking a drink. But as time goes on and I see how much better my life is, it gets easier. I believe now that I have no more reservations, no idea in the back of my mind that some day I'll be able to drink safely.

Third, I had to be absolutely honest with myself and with other people. I had to take an inventory of myself and admit the wrongs I had done. I had to come clean with my wife and my friends and try to make it up to them for the way I had treated them.

Fourth, I had to turn to a Higher Power for help. I think that most of us, especially if we think of ourselves as agnostics, do this as a last resort, having tried everything else first. But when I tried it, I found that it worked. It's been proved that the belief in a Higher Power can keep a man or woman sober. The thousands of people in AA who are sober today are the proof. Each man or woman you see in AA is a demonstration of the power of God to change a human being from a drunkard to a sober, useful citizen. This Higher Power is keeping me from drinking and it'll keep me sober as long as I seek God's help.

Fifth, I had to live one day at a time. I start each day with a few minutes of reading, meditation, and prayer. I ask God to give me the power to stay sober for the next twenty-four hours. If I don't take that first drink today, I'll never take it, because it's always today. I like the old saying: "Yesterday is gone, forget it; tomorrow never comes, don't worry; today is here, get busy."

Sixth, I had to come to meetings regularly for fellowship and help. A personal witness is the thing that helps most. Hearing other alcoholics tell about their experiences with liquor, whether they are humorous or sad, keeps me from drinking. If I missed a few meetings, I'd be in danger of having a slip.

Seventh, I had to work with other alcoholics. Trying to help others takes my mind off myself and helps a lot in keeping me on the right path. It fills up the time I formerly spent on drinking. And seeing another alcoholic suffer keeps me sober. The Book told me I had these seven thing to do:

1. Admit I'm an alcoholic.
2. Realize I must spend the rest of my life without liquor.
3. Be absolutely honest with myself.
4. Turn to a Higher Power for help.
5. Live one day at a time.
6. Come to meetings regularly.
7. Work with other alcoholics.

If I keep doing these seven things, I know I'll stay sober. The AA program will never fail me as long as I don't fail it.[23]

MARCH 18
AA Thought For The Day

When a man comes into AA and faces the fact that he must spend the rest of his life without liquor, it often looks like too big an order for him. So AA tells him to forget about the future and bite it off one day at a time. All we really have is now. We have no past time and no future time. As the saying goes: "Yesterday is gone, forget it; tomorrow never comes, don't worry; today is here, get busy." All we have is the present. The past is water over the dam and the future never comes. When tomorrow gets here, it will be today. Am I living one day at a time?

Meditation For The Day

Persistence is necessary, if you are to advance in spiritual things. By persistent prayer, persistent firm and simple trust, you achieve the treasures of the spirit. By persistent practice, you can eventually obtain joy, peace, assurance, security, health, happiness, and serenity. Nothing is too great, in the spiritual realm, for you to obtain through persistently preparing yourself for it.

Prayer For The Day

I pray that I may persistently carry out my spiritual exercises every day. I pray that I may strive for peace and serenity.[24]

Dear *Grapevine:*

I believe I was a potential alcoholic from the beginning, although I didn't actually become one until after quite a few years of drinking. I was the type that usually becomes an alcoholic. I was sort of an odd child. I had an inferiority complex. I was lonely. I didn't know how to make friends. I kept a sort of wall between myself and other people. And I took to drinking as a duck takes to water.

I believe that every alcoholic has a personality problem. He drinks to escape from life, to counteract a feeling of loneliness or inferiority, or because of some emotional conflict within himself, so that he cannot adjust himself to life. His alcoholism is a symptom of his personality disorder. And I don't believe an alcoholic can stop drinking unless he finds a way to solve his personality problem. That's why going on the wagon doesn't solve anything. That's why taking the pledge usually doesn't work. Because that fundamental personality problem is not solved by going on the wagon or by taking the pledge. In AA, an alcoholic finds a way to solve his personality problem. He does this by recovering three things.

First, he recovers his personal integrity. He pulls himself together. He gets honest with himself and with other people. He faces himself and his problems honestly instead of running away. He takes a personal inventory of himself to see where he really stands. Then he faces the facts instead of making excuses for himself. He recovers his integrity.

Second, he recovers his faith in a Power greater than himself. He admits that he's helpless by himself and he calls on that Higher Power for help. He surrenders his life to God, as he understands Him. He puts his drink problem in God's hands and leaves it there. He recovers his faith.

Third, he recovers his proper relationships with other people. He thinks less about himself and more about others. He tries to help other alcoholics. He makes new friends so that he's no longer lonely. He tries to live a life of service instead of selfishness. All his relationships with other people are improved.

I believe that if an alcoholic wants to stop drinking, he must find a way to solve his personality problem. If he follows the AA program, he recovers his personal integrity, his faith, and a way of fellowship and service to others. When his personality problem is solved, his drink problem is solved so long as he never takes that first drink.[3]

APRIL 6
AA Thought For The Day

Every alcoholic has a personality problem. He drinks to escape from life, to counteract a feeling of loneliness or inferiority, or because of some emotional conflict within himself, so that he cannot adjust himself to life. His alcoholism is a symptom of his personality disorder. An alcoholic cannot stop drinking unless he finds a way to solve his personality problem. That's why going on the wagon doesn't solve anything. That's why taking the pledge usually doesn't work. Was my personality problem ever solved by going on the wagon or taking the pledge?

Meditation For The Day

God irradiates your life with the warmth of His spirit. You must open up like a flower to this divine irradiation. Loosen your hold on earth, its cares and its worries. Unclasp your hold on material things, relax your grip, and the tide of peace and serenity will flow in. Relinquish every material thing and receive it back again from God. Do not hold on to earth's treasures so firmly that your hands are too occupied to clasp God's hands, as He holds them out to you in love.

Prayer For The Day

I pray that I may be open to receive God's blessing. I pray that I may be willing to relinquish my hold on material things and receive them back from God.[24]

MODERN MIRACLE

I think we must remember that we are offering something intangible. We are offering a psychological and spiritual program.

We are not offering a medical program. If a man needs medical treatment, we call in a doctor. If a man needs sedatives or B vitamins, we let the doctor give them to him. If a man needs hospital treatment we let the hospital take care of him. Our vital AA work starts when a man is physically able to receive it.

We are offering a psychological program. A man must be mentally able to receive it. He must have made up his mind that he wants to quit drinking and he must be willing to do something about it. Then we must get his confidence by showing him that we are his friends and we really desire to help him. When we have his confidence he will listen to us. Then follows the group therapy, the fellowship of other alcoholics who understand his problem because they have been through it themselves.

We are offering a spiritual program. The fundamental basis of AA is a belief in some Power greater than ourselves. This takes a man off the center of the universe and allows him to transfer his problems to some Power outside of himself. He turns to this Power for the strength he needs to keep sober.

Psychologists are turning to religion because just knowing about ourselves is not enough. A man needs the added dynamic of faith in a Power outside of himself on which he can rely. As I see it, books on psychology and psychiatric treatments are not enough without the strength that comes from faith in God.

Ministers and priests are turning to psychology because faith is an act of the mind and religion must be explained in psychological terms to satisfy the modern man. Faith must be built on our own psychological experience.

We are offering an intangible thing—a psychological and spiritual program. The newcomer must turn to a Higher Power, with faith that that Power can give him the strength he needs. Then he must re-educate his mind by learning to think along new lines. The man who achieves sobriety through faith and mental education is a modern miracle. The function of AA is to produce modern miracles.[3]

AUGUST 7
AA Thought For The Day

We in AA are offering an intangible thing, a psychological and spiritual program. It's a wonderful program. When we learn to turn to a Higher Power, with faith that that Power can give us the strength we need, we find peace of mind. When we re-educate our minds by learning to think differently, we find new interests that make life worthwhile. We who have achieved sobriety through faith in God and mental re-education are modern miracles. It is the function of our AA program to produce modern miracles. Do I consider the change in my life a modern miracle?

Meditation For The Day

You should never doubt that God's spirit is always with you, wherever you are, to keep you on the right path. God's keeping power is never at fault, only your realization of it. You must try to believe in God's nearness and the availabililty of His grace. It is not a question of whether God can provide a shelter from the storm, but of whether or not you seek the security of that shelter. Every fear, worry, or doubt is disloyalty to God. You must endeavor to trust God wholly. Practice saying: All is going to be well. Say it to yourself until you feel it deeply.

Prayer For The Day

I pray that I may feel deeply that all is well. I pray that nothing will be able to move me from that deep conviction.[24]

WE ARE TWO PEOPLE
Do Alcoholics Have A "Wet Subconscious"?

In the article "Ninety Days Will Do It" in the July *Grapevine*, this statement is made: "As a mental factor, it should by now be limited to the subconscious where day by day new walls of defense are built around it, to prevent it from taking over any conscious act." Also this statement: "Until alcohol as a means of escape . . . leaps from the subconscious to the conscious and the resulting . . . thirst is a natural reaction." I heartily agree with the phraseology.

The fact is, *I believe that our subconscious minds will be alcoholic as long as we live.* For example, I have been dry for quite a few years, yet when I am asleep, I still occasionally dream that I am drunk. These dreams are a result of my wet subconscious mind.

A *wet subconscious* is the reason that an alcoholic is never cured, nor does it seem likely that a cure for alcoholism will be found, because no physical treatment can change the wet subconscious mind. When does a person become an alcoholic? When his conscious and subconscious mind have been thoroughly conditioned that he cannot take one drink without setting in motion the mental processes that lead to drunkenness. In AA, we substitute a way of thinking that makes the conscious mind resistant to drinking. Our spiritual program allows the Higher Power to take over the workings of our conscious minds. But as our subconscious minds are similar to that of the lower animals, it seems impossible for a thoroughly conditioned subconscious mind to be changed from wet to dry. The theory of a wet subconscious has its advantages. It makes the AA program a never-ending one. With the help of God, we make a constant daily effort to keep the conscious mind in good condition, by building new walls of defense to prevent the subconscious mind from taking over. Our old way of thinking can so often leap from the subconscious to the conscious. We must be very careful about daydreaming or wishful thinking.

The theory of the *wet subconscious* also explains slips, which sometimes occur even after several years of sobriety. The thoughts that come before taking a drink are often largely subconscious. The person usually doesn't know consciously what made him do it. Our subconscious minds may never become free from alcoholic thoughts as long as we live, but when, through our spiritual program, our conscious minds are fully conditioned against drinking, we can stay sober and our subconscious minds do not often bother us. We shudder when a man says: "I'll never take another drink as long as I live." How does he know? His wet subconscious mind is always there, ready to take over if he ever lets down the bars of his conscious dry thinking.

An idle thought connected with drinking casually pops into my mind. This is the crucial moment. Will I harbor that thought even for one minute or will I banish it from my mind at once? If I let it stay, it may develop into a daydream. If I allow the daydream to stay in my mind, it may lead to a decision, however unconscious, to take a drink. Then I am headed for a slip. As long as we live, we must be on the lookout for such thoughts and guard against them. In fact, our AA spiritual training is largely to prepare us for this eventuality, to make us able to recognize such thoughts at once and to reject them at once.

The AA program is largely one of spiritual training. With the help of God, we must fill our mind with constructive thoughts. The length of our sobriety is not as important as the quality of it. A man who has been a member of AA for a number of years may not be in as good spiritual condition as a man who has only been in a few months. We must realize that as long as we live, we are only one drink away from a drunk. Temptation comes as a result of our neglect of the spiritual program of constructive thinking to such an extent that the wet subconscious has a chance to take over the dry conscious mind.

The theory of the *wet subconscious* is nothing to be discouraged about. It simply means that we must practice the AA spiritual principles in all our affairs as long as we live. This means regular attendance at meetings, no graduation from AA, no diplomas, no over-confidence, and no letting down the spiritual control of our character defects which, if allowed, will weaken our conscious control and allow the wet subconscious to take over.[3]

DECEMBER 8
AA Thought For The Day

The length of time of our sobriety is not as important as the quality of it. A man who has been in AA for a number of years may not be in as good mental condition as a man who has only been in a few months. It is a great satisfaction to have been an AA member for a long time and we often mention it. It may sometimes help the newer members, because they may say to themselves, if he can do it I can do it. And yet the older members must realize that as long as they live they are only one drink away from a drunk. *What is the quality of my sobriety?*

Meditation For The Day

"And greater works than this shall ye do." We can do greater works when we have more experience of the new way of life. We can have all power we need from the Unseen God. We can have His grace and His spirit, to make us effective as we go along each day. Opportunities for a better world are all around us. Greater works can we do. But we do not work alone. The power of God is behind all good works.

Prayer For The Day

I pray that I may find my rightful place in the world. I pray that my work may be made more effective by the grace of God.[24]

THE TRUE "STILL WATERS"

Alcoholics Anonymous does much more than help us to stop drinking. It shows us how to live in peace. It puts our lives in tune with Life, in harmony with God, the Power behind all life. When a man honestly faces life without liquor, he begins to find a true inner peace. Within the secret place of his being, he begins to find security and the strength to face whatever life has to offer. These are the true "still waters," beside which we are led by the hand of God. Our souls are restored.[3]

DOES AA HAVE STAYING POWER?

An editorial in the AA *Grapevine*, Vol. V, No. 11, states: "What about the member who experiences a slip after he has been in AA for several years and who has apparently assimilated its teachings thoroughly? What caused his slip? Was the knowledge at hand insufficient to help him beyond a certain period? Can additional knowledge be made available which will extend AA's help out into the broader fields that many of its members have now reached? How to extend AA's practical assistance is both a question and a challenge." This editorial was published in April, 1949, and now eight years later, the question remains unanswered—at least in a completely satisfactory way.

The broad question remains: Has AA staying power? Will it enable a person to remain on the program up to the end of his life?

The obvious answer is yes, if he continues the AA habit: "to practice these principles in all our affairs."

Certain things, however, seem to work against the continuance of our practice of the AA principles. One of them is the doctrine that AA should enable a man or woman to "live a normal life," as the saying goes; to spread out his activities in society, in community programs, in business, in hobbies, and in many other ways.

This is a perfectly good doctrine, except that so often these other activities crowd out our AA way of life and we tend to give less and less time to practicing the AA way of life and we tend to give less and less time to practicing the AA principles. A spiritual program can easily be lost in the multifarious material activities of so-called "normal living."

No doubt individuals vary considerably in this respect, but for most of us there is danger in neglecting the AA program to any great degree. Other activities can so easily assume an importance that overshadows our one great need—to keep our conscious minds full of the AA program at all times as long as we live.

The AA program consists fundamentally of fellowship, faith, and service. No one of these can be neglected without danger to our sobriety. If AA meetings are not attended regularly, fellowship can be lost. If spiritual principles are not practiced daily—by some morning quiet time, by some prayer during the day, and by the evening thanking time—faith can be lost. When any of these things happen we are in danger of falling by the wayside. Is the staying power of AA sufficient to prevent these losses?

There is one very practical answer to this question. At St. Louis in July, 1955 I talked with a girl who had held all the offices in AA (group secretary, steering committee, etc.), who had been "on the circuit" speaking at anniversaries and conventions, who had become bored at AA meetings, and who was staying away from AA activities.

This girl felt herself slipping back into the old pre-AA way of thinking. She was up against this vital question of the staying power of AA. How did she solve it? She decided to spend a couple of hours every day at her local Intergroup Office, talking with prospects and trying to help them. This she did and is still doing and is very happy in this work.

Here then is one answer for the old timer who is in danger of graduating from the AA program. No one, new member or old member, is in much danger of taking a drink when he is spending at least some of this time trying to help other alcoholics.

I have had a similar experience. Retired after thirty years in business, finding a lot of time on my hands, and being somewhat of an "old-timer" in AA, I spend each weekday morning at the local Intergroup Office. An opportunity to talk with people whose troubles are greater than mine strikes me as most effective in keeping an "old-timer" sober and happily on the program.

If you have lost some of your enthusiasm for AA; if you feel that other things in life are becoming more important than your AA way of life—try going where you can talk to somebody who needs help and you will find the best answer to the staying power of AA. Fellowship and faith are important, but continuing service to your fellow alcoholic will most surely give you the staying power you need to remain happily sober.[3]

XI. SLOGANS

SLOGANS

1. Easy Does It
2. First Things First
3. Live and Let Live
4. But for the Grace of God
5. Think . . . Think . . . Think
6. One Day At A Time
7. Let Go and Let God
8. K.I.S.S.—Keep It Simple Stupid
9. Act As If . . .
10. This Too Shall Pass
11. Expect Miracles
12. I Can't . . . He Can . . . I Think I'll Let Him
13. If It Works . . . Don't Fix It
14. Keep Coming Back . . . It Works If You Work It
15. Stick With The Winners
16. Keep Right Size
17. Sobriety Is A Journey, Not A Destination
18. Faith Without Works Is Dead,
19. Poor Me . . . Poor Me . . . Pour Me Another Drink
20. To Thine Own Self Be True
21. I Came; I Came To; I Came To Believe
22. Live In The NOW
23. If God Seems Far Away, Who Moved?
24. Turn It Over
25. AA=Altered Attitudes
26. Nothing Is So Bad, A Drink Won't Make It Worse
27. We Are Only As Sick As Our Secrets
28. There Are No Coincidences In AA

29. Be Part Of The Solution, Not The Problem
30. Sponsors: Have One—Use One—Be One
31. I Can't Handle It God; You Take Over
32. Keep An Open Mind
33. It Works—It Really Does!
34. Willingness Is The Key
35. More Will Be Revealed
36. You Will Intuitively Know
37. You Will Be Amazed
38. No Pain . . . No Gain
39. Go For It
40. Keep The Plug In The Jug
41. Do It Sober
42. Let It Begin With Me
43. Just For Today
44. Sober 'n' Crazy
45. Pass It On
46. It's In The Book
47. You Either Is—Or You Ain't
48. Before You Say: I Can't . . . Say: I'll Try
49. Don't Quit 5 Minutes Before The Miracle Happens
50. Some Of Us Are Sicker Than Others
51. We're All Here Because We're Not All There
52. Alcoholism Is An Equal Opportunity Destroyer
53. Practice An Attitude Of Gratitude
54. The Road To Sobriety Is A Simple Journey For Confused People With A Complicated Disease
55. Another Friend Of Bill W.'s
56. God Is Never Late
57. Have A Good Day Unless You've Made Other Plans
58. Decisions Aren't Forever

59. It Takes Time
60. 90 Meetings 90 Days
61. You Are Not Alone
62. Wherever You Go, There You Are
63. Don't Drink, Read The Big Book, And Go To Meetings
64. Use The 24-Hour Plan
65. Make Use Of Telephone Therapy
66. Stay Sober For Yourself
67. Look For Similarities Rather Than Differences
68. Remember Your Last Drunk
69. Remember That Alcoholism Is Incurable, Progressive, And Fatal
70. Try Not To Place Conditions On Your Sobriety
71. When All Else Fails, Follow Directions
72. Count Your Blessings
73. Share Your Happiness
74. Respect The Anonymity Of Others
75. Share Your Pain
76. Let Go Of Old Ideas
77. Try To Replace Guilt With Gratitude
78. What Goes Around, Comes Around
79. Change Is A Process, Not An Event
80. Take The Cotton Out Of Your Ears And Put It In Your Mouth
81. Call Your Sponsor Before, Not After, You Take The First Drink
82. Sick And Tired Of Being Sick And Tired
83. It's The First Drink That Gets You Drunk
84. To Keep It, You Have To Give It Away
85. Man's Extremity Is God's Opportunity
86. The Price For Serenity And Sanity Is Self-sacrifice

87. One Alcoholic Talking To Another
88. Take What You Can Use And Leave The Rest
89. What If . . .
90. Yeah But . . .
91. If Only . . .
92. Help Is Only A Phone Call Away
93. Around AA Or In AA?
94. You Can't Give Away What You Don't Have
95. One Drink Is Too Many And A Thousand Not Enough
96. Welcome To AA—"Keep Coming Back"
97. Anger Is But One Letter Away From Danger
98. Courage To Change . . .
99. Easy Does It, But Do It
100. Bring The Body And The Mind Will Follow
101. Accept Your Admission
102. Remember When . . .
103. Dry Up And Tighten Up (Financially)
104. We AAs Are 'Gifted' People
105. There Are 12 Steps In The Ladder Of Complete Sobriety
106. Fear Is The Darkroom Where Negatives Are Developed
107. Before Engaging Your Mouth, Put Your Mind In Gear!
108. I Want What I Want When I Want It
109. There Is No Chemical Solution To A Spiritual Problem
110. AA Is Not Something You Join, It's A Way Of Life
111. We Can Be Positive That Our Drinking Was Negative
112. Spirituality Is The Ability To Get Our Minds Off Ourselves
113. Faith Is Spelled A-C-T-I-O-N
114. Backsliding Begins When Knee-bending Stops
115. If I Think, I Won't Drink. If I Drink, I Can't Think
116. Bend Your Knees Before You Bend Your Elbow

117. The First Step In Overcoming Mistakes Is To Admit Them.
118. Formula For Failure: Try To Please Everyone
119. There's A Slip Under Every Skirt! (13th Step)
120. **Willpower** = Our **Will**-ingness To Use A Higher **Power**
121. AA Is Education Without Graduation!
122. When Your Head Begins To Swell Your Mind Stops Growing
123. A Journey Of A Thousand Miles Begins With The First Step
124. GOD=Good Orderly Direction
125. Be As Enthusiastic About AA As You Were About Your Drinking
126. You Received Without Cost, Now Give Without Charge
127. Humility Is Our Acceptance Of Ourselves
128. Trying To Pray Is Praying
129. Get It—Give It—Grow In It
130. Faith Is Not Belief Without Proof But Trust Without Reservation
131. We're Responsible For The Effort Not The Outcome
132. This Is A Selfish Program
133. EGO=Edge God Out
134. Keep Your Sobriety First To Make It Last
135. I Drank: Too Much—Too Often—Too Long
136. AA Will Work If You Want It To Work!
137. Minds Are Like Parachutes—They Won't Work Unless They're Open
138. What You Hear And See Here, Stays Here
139. Alcoholism Is The Only Disease That Tells You You're All Right

140. If You Turn It Over And Don't Let Go Of It, You Will Be Upside Down

141. An AA Meeting Is Where Losers Get Together To Talk About Their Winnings

142. AA Is A School In Which We Are All Learners And All Teachers

143. Please Lord, Teach Us To Laugh Again, But, God Don't Let Us Ever Forget That We Cried

144. Serenity Is Not Freedom From The Storm But Peace Amid The Storm

145. AA May Not Solve All Your Problems But It Is Willing To Share Them

146. It Isn't The Load That Weighs Us Down—It's The Way We Carry It

147. Principles Before Personalities

148. When You Do All The Talking You Only Learn What You Already Know

149. By Accepting God's Help We Learn To Think Clearly, To Play Fairly, And To Give Generously

150. There Are None Too Dumb For The AA Program But Many Are Too Smart

151. We All Have Another Drunk Left In Us But We Don't Know If We Have Another Recovery In Us

152. Your Wildest Dreams Will Be Realized In The AA Fellowship

153. When We Surrender To Our Higher Power, The Journey Begins

154. The Person With The Most Sobriety At A Meeting Is The One Who Got Up Earliest That Morning

155. Knowledge Of "The Answers" Never Made Anyone Slip—It Was Failing To Practice "The Answers" Known

156. What Is The Common Denominator Of AA Sobriety? Putting Sobriety Ahead Of Everything Else In Life! Put **First Things First!**

157. We Are Not Human Beings Having Spiritual Experiences; We Are Spiritual Beings Having Human Experiences

158. We In AA Don't Carry The Alcoholic; We Carry The Message. The Results Are In God's Hands

159. When We Get To The Place Where There's Nothing Left But God, We Find That God Is Enough

160. Lord Help Me To Remember That Nothing Is Going To Happen To Me Today That You And I Together Can't Handle . . .

161. When Man Listens, God Speaks; When Man Obeys, God Works.

162. Don't Watch The "Slippers" But Watch Those Who Don't Slip Closely And Watch Them Go Through Difficulties And Pull Through

163. The Three Ts Of Gratitude To Repay AA For Our Sobriety: Our Time—Our Talent—Our Treasure!

164. It's A Pity We Can't Forget Our Troubles The Same Way We Forget Our Blessings!

165. Be Careful What You Pray For; You're Liable To Get It

166. My Sponsor Told Me To "Get A Check-up From The Neck Up!"

167. The Time To Attend A Meeting Is When You Least Feel Like Going

168. We Can Act Ourselves Into Right Thinking Easier Than We Can Think Ourselves Into Right Acting

169. AA Is The Highest Priced Fraternity In The World. If You Have Paid Your Dues, Why Not Enjoy The Benefits?

170. When A Person Tries To Control Their Drinking They Have Already Lost Control

171. The First Step Is The Only Step A Person Can Work Perfectly

172. The Will Of God Will Never Take You Where The Grace Of God Will Not Protect You

173. Your Best Sponsor Is The Big Book

174. We Came To AA To Stop Drinking . . . What We Found Was A Way To Start Living

175. Serenity Or Peace Of Mind Is Accomplished By Very Few People In This World. True Happiness Will Come To The Person Who Seeks And Finds How To Serve Others

176. Whatever You Are, AA Will Make You Want To Do Better

177. AA Never Opened The Gates Of Heaven To Let Me In, AA Did Open The Gates Of Hell To Let Me Out

178. The Only Thing We Take From This World When We Leave Is What We Gave Away

179. Time Wasted In Getting Even Can Never Be Used In Getting Ahead

180. Some People Are So Successful In AA That They Turn Out To Be Almost As Good As They Used To Think They Were When They Were Drinking

181. We Who Have Done So Little With So Much Now Find That With FAITH We Can Do Anything With Nothing

182. Them Which Stops Going To Meetings Are Not Present At Meetings To Hear What Happens To Them Which Stops Going To Meetings

183. "There Is A Principle Which Is A Bar Against All Information, Which Is Proof Against All Arguments And Which Cannot Fail To Keep A Man In Everlasting Ignorance. That Principle Is Contempt Prior To Investigation."
Herbert Spencer

184. If Faith Without Works Is Dead; Then . . . Willingness Without Action Is Fantasy.

185. **AA WON'T**
Keep You From Going To Hell
Nor Is It A Ticket To Heaven
BUT IT WILL
Keep You Sober Long Enough
For You To Make Up Your Mind
Which Way You Want To Go!

186. The 12 Steps Tell Us How It Works; The 12 Traditions Tell Us Why It Works . . .

187. **Fear** Stands For:
Frustration
Ego
Anxiety
Resentment

188. **H.A.L.T.** = Don't Get Too **H**ungry . . . Or Too **A**ngry . . . Or Too **L**onely . . . Or Too **T**ired . . .

189. First We Stay Sober Because We **Have To** . . .
Then We Stay Sober Because We **Are Willing To** . . .
Finally We Stay Sober Because We **Want To** . . .

190. **Danger Sign:**
When Your Eyes Have Wandered From The Alcoholics
Who Still Suffer And Need Help—To The Faults Of
Those Whom The Program Has Already Helped!

191. Have A Ball
Without Alcohol!
Pass It Up, So You Can
Pass It On!

192. Sobriety Delivers Everything Alcohol Promised!
193. Possibilities And Miracles Are One In The Same!
194. Get Out Of The Driver's Seat—Let Go And Let God!

195. Some People That Come To AA Think It Is Just Like
Aladdin's Magic Lamp. All They Need To Do Is Just Rub
Up Against It And They'll Get Their Wish For Sobriety

196. Before I Came To AA I Had No Choice; I Had To Drink.
But Now I Have A Choice

197. IF YOU Want To Know **HOW** This Program Works,
Take The First Word Of Your Question: The **H** Is For
Honesty, The **O** Is For Open-mindedness, And The **W** Is
For Willingness: These Our Big Book Calls "The Essen-
tials Of Recovery."

198. Rationalization Is Giving A Socially Acceptable Reason For Socially Unacceptable Behavior, And Socially Unacceptable Behavior Is A Form Of Insanity.

199. For Everyone Who Asks Receives, And Those Who Seek Find, And To Those Who Knock It Will Be Opened

200. Active Alcoholics Go On What They Call "Geographics." They Pack Everything And Move Somewhere Else To Start Again . . . They Also Pack Up Their Problems And Take Them Along With Them! Because, No Matter How Fast Or Far You Run . . . You Never Seem To Get Away From Yourself

201. The Task Ahead Of Us Is Never As Great As The Power Behind Us

202. AA Works For People Who Believe In God
AA Works For People Who Don't Believe In God
AA Never Works For People Who Believe They **Are** God

203. **SIGN AT AN AA MEETING:**
Nobody Act Big
Nobody Act Small
Everybody Act Medium

204. Remember—The Pursuit Of Happiness Is Futile. Happiness, Peace Of Mind, And Serenity Are The Results Of The Way **You** Think God Would Have You Live

205. **On The Beam**—Getting On With The Business Of Living—By Using AA

206. You Shall Know The Truth, And The Truth Shall Make You Free

207. We In AA Say That A "Coincidence" Is A "Miracle" In Which God Chooses To Remain Anonymous

208. Active Alcoholics Don't Have Relationships; They Take Hostages

209. If You Are New And The Laughter In This AA Meeting Puzzles You, Just Listen Real Close And You Will Hear God Saying "I Forgive You, Now Why Don't You Forgive Yourself?"

210. **Faith** Is A Lighted Doorway, But **Trust** Is A Dark Hallway Inside That Says "Do I Dare Walk This Way, Not Knowing Where It Will Lead?"

211. IF You Find Joy In Looking For Faults In People And Fellow AAs—Start With Yourself—It Will Be A Real Laugh Riot

212. **MISTAKES**
The More I Turn Outward To Others,
The Stronger I Become Within
Mistakes Are Facts Of Life,
It Is The Response To Error That Counts

213. If It Is Peace You Want, Seek To Change Yourself, Not Other People. It Is Easier To Protect Your Feet With Slippers Than To Carpet The Whole Of The Earth

214. If You Find A Path With No Obstacles, It Probably Doesn't Lead Anywhere

215. The Lesson I Must Learn Is Simply That My Control Is Limited To My Own Behavior, My Own Attitudes. Today Can Be My New Beginning

216. Live Your Life So You Will Never Have To Say . . . If Only!

217. Serenity=Reality=Inner Peace And Strength

218. Every Recovery From Alcoholism Began With One Sober Hour!

219. Each And Every Alcoholic—Sober Or Not—Teaches Us Some Valuable Lessons About Ourselves And Recovery

220. It Takes The Good And Bad AA Meeting—The Good And Bad AA Talk—To Make This Fellowship "Work"

221. Seven Days Without An AA Meeting Makes One **Weak!**

222. We Had To Quit Playing God!

223. You're Not Required To Like It, You're Only Required To **Do It!**

224. We Surrender To Win
We Die To Live
We Suffer To Get Well
We Give It Away To Keep It

225. **Rule 62**: Don't Take Yourself So Damn Seriously!

226. Don't Compare—Identify!

227. Don't Intellectualize—Utilize!

228. AA Has A Wrench To Fit Every Nut That Walks Through A Meeting Room Door!

229. Faith Is Our Greatest Gift; Its Sharing With Others Our Greatest Responsibility

230. If You Want To Drink—That's Your Business
If You Want To Quit—That's Our Business
—Call Us—
Alcoholics Anonymous

231. In A Bar, We Got Sympathy—As Long As Our Money Lasted. In AA, We Get Understanding—For Nothing!

232. Even My Worst Day In Sobriety Is Better Than My Best Day Drunk!

233. The Steps Can Only Take Us As Far As We Allow Them To Take Us

234. The Elevator Is Broken—Use The Steps!

235. Sobriety Is Like Standing Up At The Starting Line. The Race Hasn't Started Yet But At Least You're Standing Up Rather Than Lying Down!

236. The Smartest Thing An AA Member Can Say Is, "Help Me"

237. Yesterday Is Gone, Forget It; Tomorrow Never Comes, Don't Worry; Today Is Here, Get Busy!

238. Living In The Here And Now

239. The Surest Way To AA Is To Go All The Way To Hell And Make A U-turn

240. Our Need Is God's Opportunity!

241. God Will Never Give You More Than You Can Handle

242. You Are Exactly Where God Wants You To Be

243. Slow But Sure . . .

244. How Does One Become An "Old-timer"? Don't Drink And Don't Die!

245. AA Spoils Your Drinking

246. Why Recovery Never Ends: The Disease Is Alcohol*ism* Not Alcohol*wasm*!

247. When You Are A Sponsor, You Get Out Of Yourself. If I Serve, I Will Be Served

248. The AA Way Of Life Is Meant To Be Bread For Daily Use, Not Cake For Special Occasions

249. I Am Responsible For Myself Alone. My Sobriety, My Well-being, My Happiness—All Of These Are, Ultimately, My Own Responsibilities

250. Three Suggestions For Making An AA Speech:
    1. Be Interesting
    2. Be Brief
    3. Be Seated

251. There Are No Atheists In Foxholes!

252. God Gave Us Two Ears But Only One Mouth. Some People Say That's Because He Wanted Us To Spend Twice As Much Time Listening As Talking. Others Claim It's Because He Knew Listening Was Twice As Hard As Talking

253. There Is A Gentle Serenity In God's Peace—There Is A Soothing Tranquility In God's Love

254. All You Need To Start Your Own AA Meeting Is A Resentment And A Coffee Pot

255. Let It Begin With Me!

256. When All Else Fails . . . The Directions Are In The Big Book!

257. Trust God . . . Clean House . . . Help Others!

258. Anonymity Is So Important It's Half Of Our Name!

259. If We Don't Grow, We Gotta Go

260. Would I Let Anyone Do To Me What I Have Done To Myself?

261. **THE AA WAY OF LIFE**
Humble, not necessarily meek;
Accepting, not necessarily passive;
Loving, not necessarily possessive;
Honest, not necessarily ruthless;
Moral, not necessarily righteous;
Enviable, not necessarily smug;
Spiritual, not necessarily religious; and
Attractive, not necessarily irresistible

262. **12 REWARDS OF THE 12 STEP PROGRAM**
1. Hope instead of desperation
2. Faith instead of despair
3. Courage instead of fear
4. Peace of mind instead of confusion
5. Self-respect instead of self contempt

6.   Self-confidence instead of helplessness
7.   The respect of others instead of their pity and contempt
8.   A clean conscience instead of a sense of guilt
9.   Real friendship instead of loneliness
10. A clean pattern of life instead of a purposeless existence
11. The love and understanding of our families instead of their doubts and fears
12. The freedom of a happy life instead of the bondage of an alcoholic obsession

263. INSURANCE AGAINST TAKING THAT FIRST DRINK!

1.   Get a sponsor—Making sure my sponsor has a sponsor
2.   Ask for God's help in the morning
3.   Go to meetings
4.   Get involved
5.   Say "Thank You" to God every night
6.   Practice the 12 Step Principles in "All My Affairs"

264. THE MAN IN THE GLASS

When you get what you want in your struggle for self
And the world makes you king for a day,
Just go to a mirror and look at yourself,
And see what **that** man has to say.

For it isn't your father or mother or wife
Whose judgment upon you must pass;
The fellow whose verdict counts most in your life
Is the one staring back from the glass.

Some people may think you a straight-shootin' chum
And call you a wonderful guy,
But the man in the glass says you're only a bum
If you can't look him straight in the eye.

He's the fellow to please, never mind all the rest
For he's with you clear up to the end,
And you've passed your most dangerous, difficult test
If the man in the glass is your friend.

You may fool the whole world down the pathway of years
And get pats on the back as you pass,
But your final reward will be heartaches and tears
If you've cheated the man in the glass.

265. I SOUGHT MY BROTHER

I sought my soul, but my soul I could not see
I sought my God, but my God eluded me
I sought my brother, and I found all three

266. WHICH ARE YOU

There are AA members who **make** things happen
There are AA members who **watch** things happen
There are AA members who **don't know** anything
   happened
Which are you?

267. THE TWELVE PROMISES

If we are painstaking about this phase of our development,
we will be amazed before we are half way through. We are going

to know a new freedom and a new happiness. We will not regret the past nor wish to shut the door on it. We will comprehend the word serenity and we will know peace. No matter how far down the scale we have gone, we will see how our experience can benefit others. That feeling of uselessness and self-pity will disappear. We will lose interest in selfish things and gain interest in our fellows. Self-seeking will slip away. Our whole attitude and outlook upon life will change. Fear of people and of economic insecurity will leave us. We will intuitively know how to handle situations which used to baffle us. We will suddenly realize that God is doing for us what we could not do for ourselves.

Are these extravagant promises? We think not. They are being fulfilled among us—sometimes quickly, sometimes slowly. They will always materialize if we work for them.[2]

268. PUT AND TAKE
WHAT I MUST PUT IN AA
1. Complete sobriety
2. One hundred percent 12th Step work
3. Love of my fellow man
4. Attendance at the meetings, is essential to my new Way of Life
5. Giving all in my power and time to help bring in new members who have alcohol problems
6. Above all, forever as now, remaining an active member

WHAT I GET OUT OF AA
1. Peace of mind and contentment
2. The 24-hour program by which I can live a clean and decent life
3. Happiness in my home and in my daily life

4. Better citizenship
5. Better health, physically and mentally
6. Respect, not disrespect, from my fellow man
7. Many new friends
8. Blessings from God, as a result of making a decision to turn my will and life over to His care as I understand Him
9. The privilege of being an AA member forever, and this I know I am, just as long as I say I am[41]

269. 15 POINTS FOR AN ALCOHOLIC TO CONSIDER WHEN CONFRONTED WITH THE URGE TO TAKE A DRINK
-OR-
"DAILY TIPS" FOR THE OLD AND NEW AA MEMBER

The unhappiest person in the world is the Alcoholic who has an insistent yearning to enjoy life as they once knew it, but cannot picture life without alcohol. They have a heartbreaking obsession that by some miracle of control they will be able to do so.

Sobriety, the magnificent obsession, is the most important thing in your life without exception. You may believe your job, or your home life, or one of many other things come first. But consider, if you do not get sober and stay sober, chances are you won't have a job, a family, sanity, or even life. If you are convinced that everything in life depends on your sobriety, you have just so much more chance of getting sober and staying sober. If you put other things first you are only hurting your chances.

1.   Cultivate continued acceptance of the fact that your choice is between unhappy, drunken drinking and doing without just one small drink.

2.   Cultivate gratitude. You have had the good fortune of finding out what was wrong with you before it was too late.

3.   Expect as being natural and inevitable, that for a period of time, (and it may be a long one) you will recurringly experience:

(a)   The conscious, nagging craving for a drink.

(b)   The sudden, all but compelling impulse just to take a drink.

(c)   The craving, not for a drink as such, but for the soothing glow and warmth a drink or two once gave you.

4.   Remember that the times when you don't want a drink are the times in which to build up the strength not to take one when you do want one.

5.   Develop and rehearse a daily plan of thinking and acting by which you will live that day without taking a drink regardless of what may upset you or how hard the old urge for a drink may hit you.

6.   Don't for a split second allow yourself to think: "Isn't it a pity or a mean injustice that I can't take a drink like so-called normal people?"

7.   Don't allow yourself to either think or talk about any real or imagined pleasure you once did get from drinking.

8.   Don't permit yourself to think a drink or two would make a bad situation better, or at least easier to live with. Substitute the thought: "One drink will make it worse, one drink will mean a drunk."

9.   Minimize the situation. Think, as you see here or there a blind or other sorely handicapped person, how joyful

such a person would be if their problem could be solved by just not taking one drink today. Think gratefully of how lucky you are to have a simple and small problem.

10.   Cultivate the enjoyment of sobriety.

(a)   How good it is to be free of shame, mortification and self-condemnation.

(b)   How good it is to be free of fear of the consequences of a drunk just ended, or a coming drunk you have never before been able to prevent.

(c)   How good it is to be free of what people have been thinking and whispering about you, and of their mingled pity and contempt.

(d)   How good it is to be free from fear.

11.   Catalog and re-catalog the positive enjoyments of sobriety, such as:

(a)   The simple ability to eat and sleep normally, and wake up glad you are alive, glad you were sober yesterday, and glad you have the privilege of staying sober today.

(b)   The ability to face life as it is.

12.   Cultivate a helpful association of ideas:

(a)   Associate a drink as being the single cause of all the misery, shame, and mortification you have ever known.

(b)   Associate a drink as being the only thing that can destroy your new-found happiness and take from you your self-respect.

13.   Cultivate gratitude:

(a)   Gratitude that so much can be yours for so small a price.

(b)   Gratitude that you don't have to drink.

(c)   Gratitude that AA exists, and you found out about it in time.

(d)   Gratitude that you are only a victim of a disease called Alcoholism, that you aren't a degenerate, immoral weakling, or the self-elected victim of a vice, or a person of doubtful sanity.

(e)   Gratitude that since others have done it, you can in time bring it to pass that you will not want or miss the drink you are doing without.

14.   Seek ways to help other alcoholics, and remember the first way to help others is to stay sober yourself.

15.   And don't forget that when the heart is heavy and resistance is low and the mind is troubled and confused, there is much comfort in a true and understanding friend standing by. You have that friend in AA.

270. THE NEW RECRUIT

1.   They are the most important person in AA.

2.   They are not dependent on us, we are dependent on them.

3.   They are not an interruption of our work—they are the purpose of it. We are not doing them a favor by serving them—they are doing us a favor by giving us the opportunity to do so.

4.   They are a flesh and human being with feelings, emotions, and problems like our own.

5.   They are people who have failed through no fault of their own, to live the life of happiness and usefulness. We have the means and tools to rebuild their life from despair to hope, from darkness to light . . . .[42]

271. **I'M SLIPPING**

    1. When I begin to dislike AA company or conversation.

    2. When I willingly stay away from AA meetings.

    3. When I am beginning to take another person's inventory instead of mine.

    4. When I'm more afraid of being known as an AA member, than as a drunk.

    5. When I begin to remember the good times I had drinking, and overlook the bad . . .

    6. When I condemn in others that which I tolerate in myself.

    7. When I say I forgive, but don't forget.

    8. When I shrink from self-examination.

272. **LET GO, LET GOD**

To **"let go"** does not mean to stop caring, it means I can't do it for someone else.

To **"let go"** is not to enable, but to allow learning from natural consequences.

To **"let go"** is to admit powerlessness, which means the outcome is not in my hands.

To **"let go"** is not to try to change or blame another; it's to make the most of myself.

To **"let go"** is not to care for but to care about.

To **"let go"** is not to fix but to be supportive.

To **"let go"** is not to judge but to allow another to be a human being.

To **"let go"** is not to protect, it's to permit another to face reality.

To **"let go"** is not to deny but to accept.

To **"let go"** is not to nag, scold, or argue but instead to search out
  my own shortcomings and correct them.
To **"let go"** is not to adjust everything to my desires but to take
  each day as it come and cherish myself in it.

273. FORMULA FOR PEACE OF MIND

What makes one person happy and productive, and another person unhappy and frustrated? A few years ago, the
Sociology Department of Duke University did a study on
"peace of mind." Hundreds of people, both happy and unhappy,
were studied. Nine factors were found most likely to contribute
to emotional and mental stability. Note the similarity to the
principles and teachings of AA.

1.   Absence of suspicion and resentment. Nursing a
grudge was a major factor in unhappiness.

2.   Living in the present and future. Much unhappiness
stems from an unwholesome preoccupation with mistakes and
failures in the past.

3.   Not wasting time and energy fighting conditions you
can't change.

4.   Cooperating with life, instead of trying either to de-
molish it or run away from it.

5.   When you find yourself in the grip of emotional
stress, force yourself to be out-going to other people instead of
retreating within yourself and building a prison of loneliness.

6.   Refusing to pity yourself or seek self-justification in
easy alibis that make you appear "noble" to yourself and others.

7.   Cultivate the old-fashioned virtues of love, honor,
loyalty, and thrift.

8.   Stop expecting too much of yourself. When there is
too wide a gap between the standards you set for yourself and

your actual achievement, unhappiness is inevitable. If you can't improve the performance, try lowering the demands instead.

9. Find something bigger than yourself in which to believe. Self-centered, egotistical, materialistic people score lowest of all in measuring happiness.

274. YESTERDAY—TODAY—TOMORROW

There are two days in every week about which we should not worry, two days which should be kept free from fear and apprehension.

One of these days is **yesterday** with all its mistakes and cares, its faults and blunders, its aches and pains. **Yesterday** has passed forever beyond our control.

All the money in the world cannot bring back **yesterday**. We cannot undo a single act we performed; we cannot erase a single word we said . . . **yesterday** is gone.

The other day we should not worry about is **tomorrow** with its possible adversaries, its burdens, its large and poor performance. **Tomorrow** is also beyond our immediate control.

Tomorrow's sun will rise, either in splendor or behind a mask of clouds—but it will rise. Until it does, we have no stake in **tomorrow** for it is as yet unborn.

This leaves only one day . . . **today**. Any person can fight the battle of just one day. It is only when you and I add the **yesterday** and **tomorrow** that we break down.

It is not the experience of **today** that drives people mad— it is remorse or bitterness for something which happened **yesterday** and the dread of what **tomorrow** may bring.

Let us, therefore, live but One Day At A Time!

275. JUST FOR TODAY

Just for today I will try to live through this day only, and not tackle my whole life problem at once. I can do something for twelve hours that would appall me if I felt that I had to keep it up for a lifetime.

Just for today I will be happy. This assumes to be true what Abraham Lincoln said, that "Most folks are as happy as they make up their minds to be."

Just for today I will adjust myself to what is, and not try to adjust everything else to my own desires, I will take my "luck" as it comes, and fit myself to it.

Just for today I will try to strengthen my mind, I will study, I will learn something useful, I will not be a mental loafer, I will read something that requires effort, thought and concentration.

Just for today I will exercise my soul in three ways: I will do somebody a good turn, and not get found out; if anybody knows of it, it will not count. I will do at least two things I don't want to do—just for exercise. I will not show anyone that my feelings are hurt; they may be hurt, but today I will not show it.

Just for today I will be agreeable. I will look as well as I can, dress becomingly, talk low, act courteously, criticize not one bit, not find fault with anything, and not try to improve or regulate anybody except myself.

Just for today I will have a program. I may not follow it exactly, but I will have it. I will save myself from two pests: hurry and indecision.

Just for today I will have a quiet half hour all by myself, and relax. During this half hour, sometime, I will try to get a better perspective on my life.

Just for today I will be unafraid. I will enjoy that which is beautiful, and will believe that as I give to the world, so the world will give to me.

276. THIS IS AA...?

Alcoholics Anonymous is a fellowship designed and administered by a bunch of ex-drunks whose only qualification for membership is that they can't hold their booze and don't want to learn how.

It has no rules, dues or fees; nothing that any sensible organization seems to require.

At meetings, the speaker starts on one subject and winds up talking about something entirely different and concludes by saying that they don't know anything about the program except that it works.

The group is always broke, yet always seem to have enough money to carry on. They are always losing members but seem to grow. They claim AA is a selfish program but always seem to be doing something for others.

Every group passes laws, rules, edicts, and pronouncements which everyone ignores. Members who disagree with anything are privileged to walk out in a huff, quitting forever, only to return as though nothing happened and be greeted accordingly.

Nothing is ever planned 24 hours ahead, yet great projects are born and survive magnificently. Nothing in AA is according to "Hoyle." How can it survive?

Perhaps it is because we have learned to live and laugh at ourselves. **God** made man. **God** made laughter. Perhaps our Higher Power is pleased with our disorganized efforts and makes things run right no matter who pushes the wrong button. Maybe **God** is pleased, not with perfection, but because we are trying to be nobody but ourselves. We don't know how it works but it does . . . and members keep receiving their dividend checks from their AA investments.

277. **12 STEPS TO DESTRUCTION**

1. I decided I could handle alcohol, if other people would just quit trying to run my life.

2. I firmly believe that there is no greater power than myself, and anyone who says it isn't so is insane.

3. I made a decision to remove my will and my life from God, who didn't understand me anyway.

4. I made a searching and thorough moral inventory of everyone I knew, so they couldn't fool me and take advantage.

5. I sought these people out and tried to get them to admit to me, by God, the exact nature of their defects of character.

6. I became willing to help these people get rid of their defects of character.

7. I became humble enough to ask these people to remove their shortcomings.

8. I made a list of all the people who had harmed me, and waited patiently for a chance to get even with them all.

9. I got even with these people whenever possible, except when to do so would get me into trouble also.

10. I continued to take everybody's inventory and when they were wrong, **which was most of the time**, promptly made them admit it.

11. I sought through concentration of my willpower to get God, who didn't understand me anyway, to see that my ideas were best and He ought to give me the power to carry them out.

12. I have maintained my drunkenness for twenty-five years with these steps, and can thoroughly recommend them to other alcoholics who don't want to lose their hard-earned status as drunks, but wish to be left alone, to practice alcoholism in everything they do, for the rest of their lives.

278. FOOTPRINTS

One night a man had a dream. He dreamed he was walking along the beach with the Lord. Across the sky flashed scenes from his life. For each scene, he noticed two sets of footprints in the sand; one belonging to him, and the other to the Lord.

When the last scene of his life flashed before him, he looked back at the footprints in the sand. He noticed that many times along the path of his life there was only one set of footprints. He also noticed that it happened at the very lowest and saddest times in his life.

This really bothered him and he questioned the Lord about it. "Lord, you said that once I decided to follow you, you'd walk with me all the way. But I have noticed that during the most troublesome times in my life, there is only one set of footprints. I don't understand why when I needed you most you would leave me."

The Lord replied, "My precious, precious child, I love you and I would never leave you. During your times of trial and suffering, when you see only one set of footprints, it was then that I carried you."

279. IF YOU'VE HAD A SLIP

And you're back, you don't have to be consumed with shame.

The important things are:

1. You **are** back.

2. You realize you made some mistakes in the AA program.

3. Those mistakes won't be repeated. If you have had two slips and you're back, the same things apply and you are aware that you may be establishing a negative pattern. If you keep on having slips and you're back, face up to it: you are doing something very wrong and you are headed for trouble.

A recovering alcoholic is not supposed to have slips. When you are listening to a speaker talk about a slip, listen for the cause; skipping meetings, not joining a group, not sharing at meetings, running with the old crowd, not getting into the 12 Steps or whatever.

Those who make it back tell how it gets worse ... and then, there are those who don't make it back ...

280. HUMILITY

Humility is perpetual quietness of heart. It is to have no trouble. It is never to be fretted or vexed, irritable or sore; to wonder at nothing that is done to me, to feel nothing done against me. It is to be at rest when nobody praises me, and when I am blamed or despised, it is to have a blessed home in myself where I can go in and shut the door and kneel to my Father in secret and be at peace, as in a deep sea of calmness, when all around and about is seeming trouble.[43]

XII. PRAYERS

1. SERENITY PRAYER

God grant me the
SERENITY to accept the thing I cannot change,
COURAGE to change the things I can, and
WISDOM to know the difference.

2. THE LORD'S PRAYER

Our Father, who art in heaven, hallowed be Thy Name. Thy Kingdom come, Thy Will be done, on earth as it is in heaven. Give us this day our daily bread, and forgive us our trespasses, as we forgive those who trespass against us. Lead us not into temptation, but deliver us from evil. For Thine is the power and the kingdom and the glory, for ever and ever.

3. PRAYER OF SAINT FRANCIS ASSISI

Lord, make me an instrument of Your peace!
Where there is hatred—let me sow love
Where there is injury—pardon
Where there is doubt—faith
Where there is despair—hope
Where there is darkness—light
Where there is sadness—joy.
O Divine Master, grant that I may not so much seek
To be consoled as to console
To be understood as to understand
To be loved as to love
For it is in giving that we receive
It is in pardoning that we are pardoned
It is in dying that we are born to eternal life.

4. THIRD STEP PRAYER

"God, I offer myself to Thee—to build with me and to do with me as Thou wilt. Relieve me of the bondage of self, that I may better do Thy will. Take away my difficulties, that victory over them may bear witness to those I would help of Thy Power, Thy Love, and Thy Way of life. May I do Thy will always!"[2]

5. SEVENTH STEP PRAYER

"My Creator, I am now willing that you should have all of me, good and bad. I pray that you now remove from me every single defect of character which stands in the way of my usefulness to you and my fellows. Grant me strength, as I go out from here, to do your bidding.[2]

6. SANSKRIT PROVERB

Look to this day,
For it is life—
The very life of life.
In its brief course lies all
The realities and verities of existence,
The bliss of growth,
The splendor of action,
The glory of power.

For yesterday is but a dream
And tomorrow is only a vision.
But today, well lived,
Makes every yesterday a dream of happiness
And every tomorrow a vision of hope.

Look well, therefore, to this day.

7. TO BE PRAYER

O Lord, I ain't what I ought to be,
And I ain't what I want to be,
And I ain't what I'm going to be,
But O Lord, I thank You
That I ain't what I used to be.

8. TODAY'S THOUGHT

I am but one, but I am one;
I can't do everything,
But I can do SOMETHING;
What I can do, I ought to do,
What I ought to do, God helping me,—
I WILL DO.

9. TEXAS PRAYER

Our Father, we come to You as a friend.

You have said that, where two or three are gathered in Your name, there You will be in the midst. We believe You are with us now.

We believe this is something You would have us do, and that it has Your blessing.

We believe that You want us to be real partners with You in this business of living, accepting our full responsibility, and certain that the rewards will be freedom, and growth, and happiness.

For this, we are grateful.

We ask You, at all times, to guide us.

Help us daily to come closer to You, and grant us new ways of living our gratitude.[38]

10. PRAYER FOR THE HURRIED

Lord, slow me down. Ease the pounding of my heart by quieting my mind. Steady my hurried pace. Give me, in the confusion of my day, the calmness of the everlasting hills. Break the tension of my nerves and muscles.

Help me to know the magical, restoring power of sleep. Teach me to take minute vacations by slowing down to look at a flower, a cloud, to chat with a friend, to pat a dog, to read a few lines from a good book. Remind me that the race is not always to the swift; that there is more to life than increasing speed.

Let me look upward into the branches of the towering oak and know that it grew great and strong because it grew slowly and well.

Lord, slow me down . . . inspire me to send my roots deep into the soil of life's enduring values that I may grow toward the stars of my great destiny.

11. DETROIT PRAYER

Our Heavenly Father—we ask Thy blessings on this meeting. Please bless the spirit and the purpose of this group. Give us strength to follow this program according to Thy will and in all humility.

Forgive us for Yesterday, and grant us courage for Today and hope for Tomorrow.[39]

12. THANK YOU, GOD, FOR AA

Thank you, dear God, for another day;
The chance to live in a decent way;
To feel again the joy of living,
And happiness that comes from giving.
Thank you for friends who can understand
And the peace that flows from Your loving hand.
Help me to wake to the morning sun
With the prayer, "Today Thy will be done,"
For with Your help I will find the way.
Thank you again, dear God, for AA.

13. THE TWENTY-THIRD 1/2 PSALM

The Lord is my sponsor! I shall not want.

He maketh me to go to many meetings.

He leadeth me to sit back, relax, and listen with an open mind.

He restoreth my soul, my sanity, and my health;

He leadeth me in the paths of sobriety, serenity, and fellowship for mine own sake.

He teacheth me to think, to take it easy, to live and let live, and to do first things first.

He maketh me honest, humble, and grateful;

He teacheth me to accept the thing I cannot change, to change the things I can, and giveth me the wisdom to know the difference.

Yea, though I walk through the valley of despair, frustration, guilt, and remorse, I will fear no evil; for Thou art with me; Thy program, Thy way of life, the Twelve Steps . . . They comfort me.

Thou preparest a table before me in the presence of mine enemies—rationalization, fear, anxiety, self-pity, and resentment. Thou anointest my confused mind and jangled nerves with knowledge, understanding, and hope. No longer am I alone, neither am I afraid, nor sick, nor helpless, nor hopeless. My cup runneth over.

Surely sobriety and serenity shall follow me every day of my life, twenty-four hours at a time, as I surrender my will to Thine and carry the message to others. And I will dwell in the house of my Higher Power, as I understand Him, daily.

Forever and Ever.

14. THIS I BELIEVE

Tomorrow is yet to be,
But, should God grant me another day,
The Hope, Courage, and Strength
Through the working of the Twelve Steps
and Serenity Prayer,
I shall be sufficiently provided for
to meet my every need.
This I believe.

15. THERE IS NO GREATER POWER

To find direction and meaning I must tap a Higher Power. That Power is God as I understand Him. As a recovering alcoholic, I will not drink today and work the Twelve Steps as best I can. I will start each day with God and take Steps Three, Seven, and Eleven. There is no Greater Power. And then I say:

Lord, I turn my life and will over to You today.

I will walk humbly with You and my Fellow Travelers.

You are giving me a grateful heart for my many blessings. You are directing my thinking and separating me from self-pity, dishonesty, and self-seeking motives.

You are removing my resentments, fears, and other character defects that stand in my way. You are giving me freedom from self-will. Thy Will, Lord, not mine.

You will show me today what I can do to help someone who is still sick.

As I go out today to do Thy bidding, You are helping me to become a better person.

16. THE TOLERANCE PRAYER

Lord, give me tolerance toward those whose thoughts
And ways, in AA and life, conflict with mine.
For though I would, I cannot always know
What constitutes the Absolute Truth.
The other fellow may be right, while I
May be all wrong, yet unaware.
Lord, make my motives right, for only this
Can ease my conscience when I sometimes err.

Lord, give me tolerance, for who am I
To stand in judgment on another person's mistakes?
No one knows better than my inward self
How many little blunders I have and can make.
Life is full of stones that somehow trip us,
And meaning not, we stumble now and then.

Lord give me tolerance, for only You
Are rightly fit to judge my Fellow Travelers.

17. THE BEATITUDES

Blessed are the poor in spirit, for theirs is the kingdom of
    heaven.
Blessed are they that mourn, for they shall be comforted.
Blessed are the meek, for they shall inherit the earth.
Blessed are they which do hunger and thirst after righteousness,
    for they shall be filled.

Blessed are the merciful, for they shall obtain mercy.

Blessed are the pure in heart, for they shall see God.

Blessed are the peacemakers, for they shall be called the children of God.

Blessed are they which are persecuted for righteousness' sake, for theirs is the kingdom of heaven.

18. A BEGINNER'S PRAYER

Lord, I want to love You, yet I am not sure.

I want to trust You, yet I am afraid of being taken in.

I know I need You, but I am ashamed of the need.

I want to pray, but I am afraid of being a hypocrite.

I need my independence, yet I fear to be alone.

I want to belong, yet I must be myself.

Take me, Lord, yet leave me alone.

Lord, I believe; help Thou my unbelief.

Oh Lord, if You are there, You do understand, don't You?

Give me what I need, but leave me free to choose.

Help me work it out my own way, but don't let me go.

Let me understand myself, but don't let me despair.

Come unto me, O Lord—I want You there.

Lighten my darkness, but don't dazzle me.

Help me to see what I need to do, and give me strength to do it.

Lord, I believe; help Thou my unbelief.

19. OPENING PRAYER FOR AA MEETINGS

God bless this meeting and the members gathered here tonight.

Help us to make this group a haven of strength and comfort, giving to all who seek help here the beauty and friendliness of home, which shall be as a shield against temptation of all kinds and against loneliness and despair.

Bless those who are going forth from this meeting to fight the gallant fight, to know suffering; and bless those who come here to rest, those who must readjust themselves to face life once more.

20. GOD, HELP ME LIVE TODAY

God, more than anything else in this world, I just don't want to be sick anymore.

God, grant me the Serenity to accept the things I cannot change (people, places, and things), the Courage to change the things I can (my attitudes), and the common sense to know the difference.

God, help me please, stay clean and sober this day—even if it's in spite of myself.

Help me Lord, stay sensitive to my own needs and the things that are good for me, the needs of others and the things that are good for them.

And if you please, Lord, free me enough from the Bondage of Self that I may be of some useful value as a human being—

whether I understand or not. That I may carry my own keys, maintain my own Integrity and live this day at peace with You, at peace with myself, and at peace with the world I live in, just for today.

God help me in this day, demonstrate that:

It is good for me to love and to be loved.

It is good for me to understand and to be understood.

It is good for me to give and to receive.

It is good for me to comfort and to allow myself to be comforted.

And it is obviously far better for me to be useful as a human being, than it is to be a useless, senseless drunk.

God, help me please put one foot in front of the other, keep moving forward and do the best I can with what I have to work with today, accepting the results of whatever that may or may not be.

21. OH! GOD OF OUR UNDERSTANDING

This is the dawn of a new day in the AA Program. I shall thank You, my Higher Power, for last night's rest, Your gift.

Yesterday is gone, except for what I have gleaned from it—good or bad. Today, I have the same choice—a Divine privilege which swells my heart with hope and purpose. This is my day, the purity of a new beginning.

I will receive from this day exactly what I give to it. As I do good things, good will be done to me. It is my gift to mold into something everlasting and do those things which will affect the people around me in an ever-widening circle. The worthiness of this effort rests entirely with me.

This is my day for love, because I know that as I love, I will be loved. Hate and jealousy cannot exist in the presence of love. I will be sustained by this miracle of Your creation and this day will be lightened by my love for others and especially love for my Fellow Travelers in AA.

Today I will do my best without thought of failures of the past or anxieties for the future. When this day is ended, I will have no regrets. On retiring I shall thank You, my Higher Power, for this wonderful day.

22. THE ALCOHOLIC'S PRAYER

God grant me the serenity to accept my alcoholism gracefully and humbly. Grant me also the ability to absorb the teachings of Alcoholics Anonymous which by its past experience is trying to help me. Teach me to be grateful for AA's help. Guide me, Father of Light, in the path of tolerance and understanding of my fellow AAs and fellow man. Guide me away from the path of criticism, intolerance, jealousy, and envy of my friends. Let me not prejudge, let me not become a moralist, keep my tongue and thoughts from malicious idle gossip. Help me to grow in stature spiritually, mentally, and morally. Grant me that greatest of all rewards, that of being able to help my fellow sufferers in their search out of the morass that has encompassed them. Above all, help me to be less critical and impatient with myself.[40]

23. THE AA PRAYER

Power greater than ourselves, as we understand You, we willingly admit that without Your help we are powerless over alcohol and our lives have become unmanageable. We believe You can restore us to sanity.

We turn our lives and our wills over to You. We have made a searching and fearless moral inventory of ourselves and we admit to You, to ourselves, and to another, the exact nature of our wrongs. We are entirely ready to have You remove these defects of character.

We humbly ask You to remove our shortcomings. We have made direct amends to all persons we have harmed, except when to do so would injure them or others. We will continue to take personal inventory and when we are wrong we will promptly admit it. We seek through prayer and meditation to improve our conscious contact with You, and pray only for knowledge of Your will for us and the power to carry it out.

Grant us the grace to carry the message of Your help unto others and to practice the principles of the Twelve Steps in all our affairs. [44]

24. PRAYERS FROM *A DAY AT A TIME*

Today I Pray

May God grant me the patience to apply those same principles of faith and acceptance which are keys to my recovery to the whole of my emotional being. May I learn to recognize the festering of my own human anger, my hurt, my frustration, my sadness. With the help of God, may I find appropriate ways to deal with these feelings without doing harm to myself or others.[25]

Today I Pray

May I know the freedom that comes with surrender to a Higher Power—that most important kind of surrender that means neither "giving in" nor "giving up" but "giving over" my will to the will of God. Like a weary fugitive from spiritual order, may I stop hiding, dodging, running. May I find peace in surrender, in the knowledge that God wills that I be whole and healthy and He will show me the way.[25]

Today I Pray

May I give over my life to the will of God, not to the whims and insensitivities of others. When I counted solely on what other people did and thought and felt for my own happiness, I became nothing more than a cheap mirror reflecting others' lives. May I remain close to God in all things. I value myself because He values me. May I have my being in His Being and be dependent only upon Him.[25]

25. SEARCH FOR SERENITY

The search is yours and mine.
Each finds his way with help,
But yet alone.

Serenity is the goal.
It comes to those who learn to wait and grow;
For each can learn to understand himself
And say, "I've found a joy in being me,
and knowing you;
A knowledge of the depths I can descend,
A chance to climb the heights above my head."

The way is not so easy all the time.
Our feet will stumble often as we go.
A friend may need to give some extra help,
As we once gave to others
When in the hour of fear.
This is no picnic path that we have found;
But yet compared to other days
And other times,
It seems a better route.

We lost our way before,
In fear,
And guilt,
Resentments held too long.

Self-pity had its way with us;
We found the perfect alibi
For all our faults.

We do not know what life may bring
From day to day.
Tomorrow is a task not yet begun,
And we could fail to pass its test.

But this will wait,
While in Today we do the best
We can.
Today we try to grow.
Today we live,
We seek to know,
To give,
To share,
With You.[26]

26. PRAYER FOR THE VICTIMS OF ADDICTION

O blessed Lord, You ministered to all who came to You: Look with compassion upon all who through addiction have lost their health and freedom. Restore to them the assurance of Your unfailing mercy; remove from them the fears that beset them; strengthen them in the work of their recovery; and to those who care for them, give patient understanding and persevering love.

XIII. STEPS & TRADITIONS

AA PREAMBLE

Alcoholics Anonymous is a fellowship of men and women who share their experience, strength and hope with each other that they may solve their common problem and help others to recover from alcoholism.

The only requirement for membership is a desire to stop drinking. There are no dues or fees for AA membership; we are self supporting through our own contributions. AA is not allied with any sect, denomination, politics, organization or institution; does not wish to engage in any controversy, neither endorses nor opposes any causes. Our primary purpose is to stay sober and help other alcoholics to achieve sobriety.[3]

I am responsible . . .
When anyone, anywhere reaches out for help, I want the hand of AA always to be there
And for that: I am responsible.[2]

This we owe to AA's Future:
To place our common welfare first;
To keep our fellowship united.
For on AA unity depends our lives;
And the lives of those to come.[2]

THE TWELVE STEPS

1. We admitted we were powerless over alcohol—that our lives had become unmanageable.

2. Came to believe that a Power greater than ourselves could restore us to sanity.

3. Made a decision to turn our will and our lives over to the care of God *as we understood Him.*

4. Made a searching and fearless moral inventory of ourselves.

5. Admitted to God, to ourselves, and to another human being the exact nature of our wrongs.

6. Were entirely ready to have God remove all these defects of character.

7. Humbly asked Him to remove our shortcomings.

8. Made a list of all persons we had harmed, and became willing to make amends to them all.

9. Made direct amends to such people wherever possible, except when to do so would injure them or others.

10. Continued to take personal inventory and when we were wrong promptly admitted it.

11. Sought through prayer and meditation to improve our conscious contact with God *as we understood Him*, praying only for knowledge of His will for us and the power to carry that out.

12. Having had a spiritual awakening as the result of these steps, we tried to carry this message to alcoholics, and to practice these principles in all our affairs.[2]

THE TWELVE TRADITIONS

1. Our common welfare should come first; personal recovery depends upon AA unity.

2. For our group purpose there is but one ultimate authority—a loving God as He may express Himself in our group conscience. Our leaders are but trusted servants; they do not govern.

3. The only requirement for AA membership is a desire to stop drinking.

4. Each group should be autonomous except in matters affecting other groups or AA as a whole.

5. Each group has but one primary purpose—to carry its message to the alcoholic who still suffers.

6.   An AA group ought never endorse, finance, or lend the AA name to any related facility or outside enterprise, lest problems of money, property, and prestige divert us from our primary purpose.

7.   Every AA group ought to be fully self-supporting, declining outside contributions.

8.   Alcoholics Anonymous should remain forever non-professional, but our service centers may employ special workers.

9.   AA, as such, ought never be organized; but we may create service boards or committees directly responsible to those they serve.

10. Alcoholics Anonymous has no opinion on outside issues; hence the AA name ought never be drawn into public controversy.

11. Our public relations policy is based on attraction rather than promotion; we need always maintain personal anonymity at the level of press, radio, and films.

12. Anonymity is the spiritual foundation of all our Traditions, ever reminding us to place principles before personalities.[2]

AN AA MEMBER'S "CREDO"

I am glad to be part of Alcoholics Anonymous, of that great fellowship which is spreading all over the world. I am only one of many AAs, but I am one. I am grateful to be living at this time, when I can help AA to grow, when it needs me to put my shoulder to the wheel and help keep the message going.

I am glad to be able to be useful, to have a reason for living, to have a purpose in life. I want to lose my life in this wonderful fellowship and so find it again. I need the AA Principles for the development of the buried life within me, that good life which I had misplaced but which I found again in AA. This life within me is growing slowly but surely, with set-backs and mistakes, but still developing. I cannot yet know what it will be, but I know that it will be good. That's all I want to know, it will be good.

AA may be human in its organization, but it is divine in its purpose. The purpose is to point me toward the God of my understanding and the good life. My feet have been set upon the right path. I feel it in the depths of my being. I am going in the right direction with my fellow travelers. The future can be safely left to my Higher Power. Whatever the future holds, it cannot be too much for me to bear. I have the Divine Power with me, to carry me through everything that may happen.

Participating in the privileges of the AA fellowship, I shall share in the responsibilities, taking it upon myself to carry my fair share of the load, not grudgingly but joyfully. I am deeply grateful for the privileges I enjoy because of my membership in this great Way of Life. It puts a responsibility on me that I will not leave undone. I will gladly carry my fair share of the burdens. Because of the joy of doing them, they will no longer be burdens but opportunities.

I shall not wait to be drafted for service to my fellow AA members, but I shall volunteer. I shall accept every opportunity to work for AA as a challenge and I shall do my best to accept every challenge and perform my service as best as I can. I will be loyal in my attendance, generous in my giving, kind in my criticism, creative in my suggestions, loving in my attitude. I will give AA my interest, my enthusiasm, my devotion, and most of all myself to the best of my ability.

We in Alcoholics Anonymous know the joy of giving. We believe that when we come to the end of our lives, it will be only the things that we have given away that we will take with us. We will take no material thing with us, but we will take with us the kind words we have said, the kind deeds we have done, the help we have given. We alcoholics, who have been helped to find AA by someone who was interested in our welfare, believe that we are under a deep obligation to pass on the AA message to others. We members of Alcoholics Anonymous believe in this with all our hearts and minds: If an active or recovering alcoholic needs our help and asks for our help: "I am my brother's keeper."

IT WORKS—IT REALLY DOES[2]

PERMISSIONS AND
REFERENCES

PERMISSIONS

Much of the material in this volume is copyrighted by other publishers and individuals, and may not be reprinted or reproduced without the permission of the owners. A complete list of the holders of the copyright, or their agents, follows. Any errors are accidental and will be corrected in future printings upon advice to the publisher.

1. Excerpt from "AA God's Instrument" pamphlet reprinted by permission of Chicago Area AA Service Office.

2. Reprinted by permission of Alcoholics Anonymous World Services, Inc. Mailing address: Box 459, Grand Central Station, New York, NY 10163.

3. Reprinted by permission of AA Grapevine, Inc. Mailing Address: Box 1980, Grand Central Station, New York, NY 10163.

4. Reprinted by permission of *Cleveland Central Bulletin*, Cleveland District Office of AA.

5. Reprinted by permission of Central Florida Intergroup Services, Inc., Winter Park, Florida.

6. Reprinted by permission of *Share*, the journal of AA in England and Wales.

7. Reprinted by permission of *Silver Dollar*, Fargo, North Dakota.

8. Reprinted by permission of *The Coastal Bender*, Corpus Christi, Texas.

9. Reprinted by permission of *Hello Central*, Los Angeles Area Central Office of AA.

    Note: Cecil C. is the author of the "Big Book" story, "Those Golden Years."

10. Excerpt of "Spiritual Milestones in A.A." Pamphlet. Available from AA of Akron Literature, P.O. Box 5218, Akron, OH 44313.

11. Excerpt from "Twelve Steps and The Older Member" booklet. Reprinted by permission of The Phenix Society. Available from The Phenix Society, Box 351, Cheshire, CT 06410.

12. Excerpt from "Toward Spirituality: The Inner Journey" by J. Dollard, © 1983. Reprinted by permission of Hazelden Foundation, Center City, Minnesota. Pamphlet available from Hazelden Educational Materials, (800) 328-9000.

13. Excerpt from "Conscious Contact: Partnership with a Higher Power" by Gail N., © 1985. Reprinted by permission of Hazelden Foundation, Center City, Minnesota. Pamphlet available from Hazelden Educational Materials, (800) 328-9000.

14. Reprinted by permission of *Rebos Star*, Alaska Area Committee of AA.

15. Excerpt of talk at The 14th Gopher State Roundup, July 4, 1987, Minneapolis, Minnesota. Reprinted by permission of Doug D.

16. Reprinted by permission of *Akron Intergroup News*, Akron Intergroup Council.

17. Reprinted by permission of *Good News*, Modesto, California, The Northern California Council of AA.

18. Reprinted by permission from *Religion That Works*, S.M. Shoemaker Jr., Fleming Revell New York, 1928. Chapter 4, pp. 43-53.

19. Reprinted by permission from the October 1954 *Reader's Digest*, © 1954 by The Reader's Digest Assn., Inc.

20. Reprinted by permission from *The Medical Record*, July 19, 1939.

21. Reprinted by permission from the *New York State Journal*, © by the Medical Society of the State of New York. Vol. 44, pp. 1805-1810, 1944.

22. Reprinted by permission from the *Quarterly Journal of Studies on Alcohol*, Vol. 15, pp. 610-621, 1954, © by the

Journal of Studies on Alcohol, Inc., Rutgers Center of Alcohol Studies, New Brunswick, NJ 08903.

23. Excerpt from *For Drunks Only*, 1945. Reprint available from Hazelden Educational Materials, (800) 328-9000.

24. Reprinted by permission from *Twenty-Four Hours A Day* by Richmond Walker © 1975 (original 1954) by Hazelden Foundation, Center City, Minnesota. Available from Hazelden Educational Materials, (800) 328-9000.

25. Reprinted by permission from *A Day At A Time*, © 1976 by CompCare Publications, Minneapolis, Minnesota, (800) 328-3330.

26. Reprinted by permission from *Search For Serenity*, © by Lewis F. Presnall, 1959. Published by U.A.F. Salt Lake City, Utah. Available from Hazelden Educational Materials, (800) 328-9000.

27. Excerpt from "Articles Written by Dave S." Reprinted by permission of "Mirus" Intergroup Assoc. of Minneapolis, Minnesota.

28. Reprinted by permission of *The Triangle*, Montana Area Allied Alcoholics Anonymous.

REFERENCES

29.   C.G. Jung in *Man and God*.
30.   Ruth Ann H., Hughesville, MD.
31.   Anonymous, Akron, OH 1943.
32.   Jack A.H., Edgelake, OH 1951.
33.   Jacquie O., Clarkston, GA.
34.   Anonymous, Chicago, IL 1950.
35.   L.O., Anchorage, AK.
36.   P.T., Santa Clara, CA.
37.   Anonymous, Chicago, IL 1953.
38.   Larry J., Houston, TX 1940.
39.   Anonymous, Detroit, MI 1945.
40.   Anonymous, Chicago, IL 1949.
41.   Salisbury AA Group, NC 1947.
42.   Waterloo Group, IA 1946.
43.   Inscription on Dr. Bob's desk plaque.
44.   Opening AA meeting prayer, Miami, FL 1943

Inquiries, orders, and catalog requests
should be addressed to:

Glen Abbey Books, Inc.
P.O. Box 31329
Seattle, Washington 98103

Toll-free 24-hour Order Line
1-800-782-2239
(All U.S.)

FAX Line:
(206) 632-0353